TWO TALES WAGGIN'

TWO TALES WAGGIN'

A JOURNEY THROUGH GRIEF TO GRACE

PEGGY SIMMONS WILSON, PHD

PALMETTO
PUBLISHING
Charleston, SC
www.PalmettoPublishing.com

Hardcover CL ISBN: 979-8-8229-3875-5
Paperback ISBN: 979-8-8229-3876-2

To my Heavenly Father,
who sustained me;
my husband,
who encouraged me;
my dog, Coco,
who inspired me;
and my deceased loved ones,
whose memories I will forever cherish

"For it is by grace you have been saved,
through faith—and
this is not from
yourselves, it is the
gift of God—"
Eph 2:8 (NIV)

CONTENTS

PROLOGUE

"I really wanted to talk to you when we were in high school, but I knew you wouldn't want to talk to me. I was too poor for you." Those words stung and almost brought tears to my eyes. They were spoken by one of my friends when we greeted each other recently at a high school alumni reunion weekend. I was shocked that anyone would think that I harbored such feelings.

"How could you think such a thing?" I responded, fighting the tears that were determined to trickle down my cheeks. "Didn't you know how poor I was?"

That exchange reignited my desire to complete a story that I had started writing eight years prior. My friend grew up thinking he was inferior because he grew up on the wrong side of the tracks. (He is now a well-known, highly respected clergyman.) He had no idea that I felt the same way. I shared some of the challenges I faced growing up in a poor, unstable family. I explained that I was the product of all of the people who nurtured and supported me along the way.

I agonized about this encounter long after the weekend ended. It had been more than forty years since we graduated high school. I could not believe that this classmate, who sat beside me in a number of classes, held this view of my existence for so many years. So many emotions flooded my soul. An overwhelming sadness consumed me. Why was I so upset about this? Over the course of the months that followed, I spent many hours praying and meditating and remembering, in an attempt to answer this question. I knew that individuals I worked with or socialized with over the years had misconceptions about my background—assuming that I was middle class. But it never occurred to me that people I grew up with, who were a part of the village that I lived in, thought I was something that I wasn't. This awareness intensified my determination to tell my story.

In retirement, I had already begun thinking a lot about legacy—whether or not I had one, and what would I want it to be. A church that I sometimes attend has a saying: If our community doesn't change because we're here, we might as well pack up and go home. That can also apply to our lives. It matters to me that my existence on this earth made a difference. Consequently, I want my legacy to be authentic, not reimagined or an illusion. Sharing some of the struggles and tragedies that have influenced my life is, in part, an attempt to achieve that goal. It is important to me that my family and close friends appreciate me for who I am—by the grace of God, not who they perceive me to be.

When I had to put my beloved dog Coco down, I was devastated. He had been my companion and confidante for over fourteen years. I couldn't envision not having him in my life. My grief was heavy, and I wanted and needed to do something to honor Coco's memory. Writing about our lives together seemed a natural response, since putting my thoughts down on paper had always been therapeutic in times of distress. Journaling about my loss led me to think about all of the losses I had endured—not just the death of Coco and other loved ones, but of security, self-worth, self-esteem, self-confidence, love, self-control, and many other qualities that enrich our lives.

The title of the book and the idea to have Coco help me tell my story flowed from the Holy Spirit during my prayer time. Although it has taken me more than a decade, I knew I had to get it done. God's timing is not my timing. He wants someone to read it and be blessed. Grief was, and still is, a central character in my life. The events of my life depicted in this book portray the grief experiences from a multitude of losses that, in some measure, shaped who I am today. Ultimately, this book is a creative narrative based on real-life events about how my faith and my precious dog Coco helped me to navigate the wave of emotions—the fear, the shame, the guilt, the loneliness—that accompany grief and trauma and led me to grace.

GO WITH THE FLOW

Lying flat on my belly with my body stretched out, my chin pressed against the cool floor of my tiny cage (my favorite position when I'm checking things out), and my eyes circling the room, I see his shadow. Raising my head a little, I see his body. I don't know him, but he's here a lot. He never talks to me, but sometimes he tickles me under my chin. A lot of times, he just stares and smiles. (I can't believe I let him touch me without making a fuss.) But there is something about him—like I knew him from before. He's not like the others who pass by my cage: the ones who stop and make those funny "ooh-aah" sounds, trying like crazy to get me to bark or wag my tail. If they sounded like nice people, I'd lift my head from the floor and jump up on the side of my cage to play. If not, I kept as still as a mouse, looking down at the floor, hoping they would soon go away.

The man who never talks never hangs around long enough to get my attention. Guess he knows I need my space. I guess he needs his too. But who is this man? What does he want? Why is he here all the time? And what about the man who's always with him, the one with hair like mine around his chin who never says a word? Are they planning to sneak me outta here? I'm getting worried.

The funny thing is, I am beginning to like him. He reminds me of myself—a little slow coming around. But what's the point? Maybe he just comes by to get me going.

One time, I decided to take matters into my own hands. When he stopped near my cage, I jumped up on my short hind legs, rested my body on the side of my cage, looked him dead in the eyes, and barked like a crazy dog.

I would give up a treat to see that look on his face again—and they know how much I love treats around here. His eyes got so big! The man with the hair on his chin moved far away from my cage. But I wouldn't stop. I kept barking until the pretty little lady who gives me my food gave me a treat to shut me up.

"Would you like a cookie?" Her voice was music to my ears. I love cookies so much that I forgot about the man. Hard cookies, soft cookies, round cookies, flat cookies—I love them all! Grabbing the cookie from her fingers, I went to my favorite corner in my cage. She smiled at the man and walked away. When I looked up, after licking the last few crumbs of my cookie from the floor, he was gone.

After another exhausting day at work, I nearly dragged myself out of my car and into the house, where I collapsed on the nearest chair. It had been a long week. And with February being one of the coldest months of the year, the days seemed even longer. There were still four months left before the end of the school year. I wondered how I would make it through.

Thankfully it was Friday, and I didn't have to cook. I had eaten a very late lunch, so I didn't have an appetite for dinner. My husband, Cliff, and his brother, John, were taking their daily walk at the mall. I hoped they would grab a bite to eat at one of the venues in the food court. Cliff needed to walk often to maintain his strength. His chronic illness had limited most of his other activities to such a great extent. My brother-in-law was a godsend! He made sure to schedule his day so that he could accompany Cliff on his walks. John was the older brother, by two or three years, and was very protective of Cliff. I was grateful that John and his family lived only a few houses down the street from us, especially now. Cliff needed John, and so did I.

Kicking off my shoes, I sank my body deeper into the pillows on the chair, trying to find the right position to relax. My mind went quickly to thoughts about Cliff's upcoming fifty-seventh birthday. March 2 was not far away, and I had not decided on a gift. I wanted to surprise him with something really special. And I needed John's help more than ever.

In the past, Cliff loved getting all dressed up in one of his best suits for his birthday. He delighted in receiving a nice shirt, a sweater, or a great tie to wear on his dress-up occasions. But he wasn't doing much dressing up these days. So my usual gift of something to wear was out of the question. Everything I thought of getting him seemed so inappropriate—so unfitting.

John suggested I get a dog. Somehow, that didn't seem to be the right thing to do either. We'd had several dogs during our marriage. (Cliff owned a beautiful little golden-haired cocker spaniel named Princess when we first met. She was the joy of his life.) Each time we faced putting one of them down, my husband was quiet for days. He was heartbroken when we lost our most recent pet, Rusty, our beloved chow, and insisted he never wanted another dog. It hurt too much.

Nevertheless, my brother-in-law was determined. "When we go for our walks at the mall," he persisted, "we always stop by the pet store to see this furry little puppy with the sad eyes. You just gotta see him. Cliff loves watching him."

Most of the time, John was soft spoken and so laid back and so quiet. His excitement about this little puppy was certainly not characteristic of his personality. However, I wasn't convinced. What if Cliff was not able to take care of a puppy? I was already too busy to take on any more responsibilities. Doggy duty would definitely not fit into my schedule.

Having already spent too many sleepless nights worrying about this birthday gift, I wanted it all to end. Preparing to have another night of tossing and turning, I found my way to the bedroom and decided to take a nap before Cliff returned home. Lying across the bed, I pulled the warm blanket at the foot of the bed up over my head to shield the light coming through the window and whispered a prayer: "Dear Lord, please help me." Closing my eyes, I asked for sleep. Seconds later, my spirit whispered, "A dog is exactly what he needs." I smiled. "Thank you," I said out loud. God had answered my prayer. I closed my eyes again and slept.

Early the next morning while Cliff was still asleep, I called John. "Okay. Show me the puppy!" I exclaimed in delight before he could say hello. A few hours later, we were headed to the mall.

The sitters are busy with our potty rounds and feeding us grain bowls. After licking up the crumbs next to my bowl, I roll on my back and swish back and forth on the floor like a windshield wiper.

Flipping over on my belly, I stretch out one last time before getting started—watching humans go in and out. It looks like one of those busy times when lots of people will pass my cage and try to get a rise out of me. I can tell by the noise. I have to be ready!

I'm already in my favorite position when my eyes spot two people talking to the pretty lady who gives me my treats. Why are they looking my way? Hey! Wait a minute! I recognize that man! He's the man who always comes in with Grand Master, but never says a word! (Oh yeah... I chose the name Grand Master for the man who stops by my cage all the time. There is something about him. He reminds me of someone who is always in charge...like me.) Who is the lady with him? Where is Grand Master? My ears perk up, trying to hear what they are saying.

"Why don't you both go over for a visit while I check his papers?"

The store clerk seemed eager for us to make a decision. She was a sweet, young girl who had only been working at the pet store for a short while. She looked like a schoolgirl dressed in her tight jeans and motley, oversized T-shirt. When we told her we wanted to spend some time with the pup, she assured us we could spend all the time we wanted with him—even take him for a short walk.

Heading over to the little puppy's cage, I could feel my heart flutter. This precious little one, covered in too much fur for his body, in a cage that appeared too small for him, was lying on his belly with his chin pressed to the floor in a statue-like pose. He was motionless, moving only his big, beautiful, dark-brown eyes, which swept from side to side as they tracked everyone who passed by his cage. He looked so sad, as if he thought no one would ever take him home. I'd bet it was those eyes that had captured my husband's attention. Cliff had a soft side to him that he rarely let others see, but when it came to dogs, he wore his heart on his sleeve. I felt so relieved. I was finally persuaded this was the right gift.

Soon, the store clerk joined us. We agreed to spend some time getting to know the little guy outside his cage. She escorted us into a playroom the size of a small closet, equipped with two blue metal chairs and no window.

"I'll get your little guy," she said, walking out of the room.

My palms were sweaty with excitement as I thought about what we were about to do. I knew this was the right thing. I just hoped my husband liked this little puppy as much as I did—John said he would.

Hey! Where are you taking me? I can't believe this pretty lady is moving me out of my cage! I already had my morning walk, and I am waiting for my bowl. She's gotta know it's almost lunchtime!

My ears are burning trying to hear what the lady is saying to me. I hear something about "coming with her" and "some special people." What special people? Who is she talking about? The two people who were here left in a hurry. Didn't even say goodbye. There are no more people. Humans are so confusing! I squirm and wiggle, but I can't shake myself loose from that tight grip of hers. Tiring myself out, I decide to go with the flow. There are times when we have no choice but to let humans be alphas.

The store clerk returned to the room with the cute little puppy snuggled under her arms. She placed him carefully on the floor, gave him a quick pat on his head, and left us alone with him to get acquainted.

"And you be a good little boy," she said, wagging her skinny finger at the puppy as she left the room.

John picked him up so we could get a good look at him. He resembled a ball of pecan-tan fur the size of a coconut. His dark eyes looked out of place as they fought to be seen amid such soft and fine hair. I fondled his cute floppy ears, checking for any sign of bruises or sores while John was holding him.

Getting restless, the little pup tried to wiggle his way out of John's hands. I was quick to catch him as he was about to fall to the floor and gently put him down next to me. (We later discovered that this little guy did not like being held. But he loved cuddling—mostly with me.) He immediately pounced on my feet and began gnawing ferociously at the white shoelaces in my sneakers. I walked playfully around the tiny visiting room while the puppy scooted along quickly to keep up with me, refusing to let go of those shoelaces. When he seemed to be getting tired of this game, I picked him up. To my surprise, he did not pull away as before but snuggled into my arms, pressing his little forehead into my chest. My heart fluttered. I was in love!

What's happening? I can't believe the pretty lady is leaving me alone with these people! Do you see the size of that man's hands? They are almost as big as the dog's head in the cage next to mine, the dog that tries to squeeze his paws through my cage to grab my cookies. He'd

better be glad I'm able to calm myself down by chewing on those shoelaces. Something's strange! He looks like the man who's always with Grand Master, except for those hands. Why is he with this lady? I'm not sure I like these people! Well, maybe the lady, but I hope they aren't planning to take me home with them. I'll protest! I wonder what happened to Grand Master.

"Yes, we want him," I said with a smile. "We want it to be a surprise, so could you please keep him here for another week? My husband's birthday is a week away, and I don't have a place to keep him without giving away the surprise."

I can't believe my doggy ears! This lady and the man with the big hands want me to surprise someone—but not now? Why let me stay in this old cage? Taking a dog home right away would be surprise enough. I sure was hoping I would be with Grand Master. But I'll try not to complain. After all, I finally have a new home. No more cage cramps!

UNEXPECTED GUEST

The more I thought about it, the more excited I became about our plan. I was really looking forward to surprising Cliff with his special birthday gift. The Holy Spirit had given a stamp of approval. I was eager to witness Cliff's reaction to seeing this little puppy's face again.

All this mystery-making reminded me of my first encounter with Cliff. We met, supposedly unexpectedly, at the home of our mutual friends, Mae and Josh. (Actually, Mae was *my* friend, and Cliff was Josh's.) To this day, I believe it was a setup. I was working as a newly hired language arts middle school teacher in a rural community in upstate New York. Mae worked as an elementary school teacher in another town, closer to the city. She often invited me to dinner on weekends to get me *out of the country*. That was the extent of my social life: back to work on Monday morning. I didn't mind the isolation so much. I was a first-year teacher who thrived on working overtime preparing creative lesson plans for my students. I didn't think much about socializing, but since cooking was neither my specialty nor my interest, I never refused a meal.

Mae and I met in the fall of 1969 while attending a small liberal arts college in North Carolina. She was a year ahead of me, so we did not see each other often. Our friendship grew when we met again in upstate New York. After having completed our teacher internships a year apart, in the suburbs of the city, both of us had accepted jobs teaching in the area.

The place where we worked was a medium-sized city in upstate New York. During the late sixties and early seventies, the practically lily-white schools in and surrounding this town were heavily recruiting minority teachers to diversify the teaching and administrative staff in the schools. Applicants who had participated in the Southern Student Teaching Program, sponsored by the Human Relations Commission in the area along with supportive Historically Black Colleges and Universities (HBCU), were given serious consideration in the hiring process. This program recruited students from southern teaching colleges to complete their student internships in predominately white-populated schools participating in the program. Some folks referred to this collaboration as an affirmative action initiative. Mae and I had been participants of that program and were grateful to have been hired.

Mae was an upbeat and positive person who had a wide, inviting smile that could light up a room. She met Josh during her student teaching assignment. Josh was also a "southern student teacher" (as we were called) at the time. They had a whirlwind romance and married shortly after Mae graduated college. Josh had also been hired the same year as an elementary school teacher. Mae taught at a suburban elementary school not far away from the city.

I didn't know Josh very well at the time. But he was always the gracious host anytime I was invited over for dinner. Josh was rather short, with a round, jovial face and a stocky build. I soon found him to be a fun-loving, talkative guy who liked making people laugh. He and Mae seemed happy together, and I enjoyed spending time with them.

Mae cooked a delicious dinner that night, featuring her famous corn pudding. She refused my request to help her clear the dinner table and insisted I sit back and relax. Soon the doorbell rang.

"Hey, man, come on in," Josh said happily, opening the door wide enough for us to see Cliff's face.

In walked this tall, handsome brown-skinned man, holding a tennis racket. He was dressed in perfectly pressed and creased white shorts—short-shorts at that—and a neatly ironed, light-colored tennis shirt. He looked a few years older than me with his nicely trimmed mustache and goatee, and he wore a short haircut, slightly longer on the top than the sides. Without telling us, Josh had invited Cliff over for a tennis match. Mae explained that Cliff and Josh were colleagues at an elementary school in the city.

"Hey, Cliff—this is Lee," Josh said, trying to hold back a chuckle.

"Hello," Cliff responded in a tone so soft, I could hardly hear him.

We chatted briefly about our jobs while Josh left the room to grab his tennis gear. After that, very little was spoken between long pauses. Mae cleared the dinner table without saying a word. I gave quick glances at her out of the corner of my eye, hoping they went unnoticed by Cliff. She kept this smile on her face, which signaled her approval. Shortly afterward, Josh and Cliff left to play a round of tennis.

"So…what was that all about?" I asked.

"What do you mean?" Mae snickered. "I didn't know Josh had invited him over."

Looking at her suspiciously, I decided to change the subject. "Let me help you in the kitchen."

We both smiled and walked toward the dining area. Putting the dishes away, we had a great time reminiscing about our college days. We always enjoyed spending time together. Mae's bubbly personality and her positive spirit were infectious, and her faith in God was encouraging. She never shied away from talking about her relationship with Jesus Christ. I loved listening. Time seemed to have flown by while we listened to some of our favorite songs on a cassette player and flipped through an old album of pictures taken while we were in college.

It wasn't too long before we heard Josh and Cliff teasing each other about who had the best game as they entered the front door of the apartment.

"Back early," Mae whispered. "Something's up."

"I hope it's not what I think," I whispered back. I didn't mind meeting new people, but dating was the last thing on my mind. I didn't need stress.

As Cliff made his way to the couch in the den where we were sitting, Josh, who appeared to be quite anxious, motioned me into the kitchen.

"Cliff wants to invite you out to dinner. He wants to know if you will go out with him."

"I-I-I don't know. I don't really know him."

"He's a nice guy. Give him a shot," Josh insisted.

"Why doesn't he ask me out himself?"

"He's a little on the shy side."

"I need to think about it, Josh. You can give him my number, and if he calls me, I'll make my decision." I felt pressured to respond in a polite manner.

Josh hurried back into the den and motioned Cliff toward the door—like two schoolboys about to get into trouble. It was all contrived. I chuckled at the thought of Josh playing this mysterious matchmaker. He was definitely out of character.

Cliff called the very next day. After a long phone conversation, I decided to go to dinner with him. Other dates followed. From the start, Cliff appeared to be smitten. I was still adjusting to the idea of dating again. I liked eating out, and Cliff always wanted to take me to the best restaurants. He teased that I only wanted to go to an eatery serving hot dogs (a southern girl's favorite menu item). Always a perfect gentleman, he made sure I was comfortable with his plans whenever we went out together. Cliff was also very generous: quick to buy me flowers and beautiful gifts on special occasions, like my birthday or Christmas. So much had happened since our first meeting. So much time had passed.

RAZZLE-DAZZLE

I'm beginning to like this lady a lot! She came back for me and bought me a brand-new crate, big enough for me to stretch out and play lots of games. She left me and the crate at the man's house with the big hands. He didn't live far from the nice lady, making it easy for her to check on me. She said he would bring me home for the surprise. The lady called me the grand finale! I don't really know what that is, but is sounds like something good! All of this excitement is making my little tail wag so hard, it's getting sore from hitting the side of my cage. I wish I could meet this man before showing up as a surprise. What if the lady made a mistake? What if he doesn't want me? Just thinking about it gives me the urge to go potty. Sometimes, crates can be a pup's best friend!

Cliff's special day had finally arrived! He was such a proud man. I didn't want to burden him by inviting too many people to the birthday party, so I decided to keep the list short: John, his wife, and their four children; his friend and colleague Cleave and his wife, Jean; his goddaughter, Rachel, and her brother. This group had become our support system, especially my friend Jean, who made sure we always had food to eat. She loved cooking and knew how tired I was after working all day. I loved her for loving us in such a special way. Jean and Cleave also gave us the joy of our lives, our goddaughter, Rachel. Asking Cliff and me to be Rachel's godparents when she was born meant so much to us. Jean and I had only known each other for a short time, but there was an immediate connection. We were now family.

I knew Cliff would be so happy to see everyone. Strangely enough, ever since Cliff's illness, he delighted in having parties. He said they helped him remain positive and hopeful. But lately, he was not himself—more tired and a little cranky. I knew how much effort it took for him to put his best face forward. A small, intimate gathering would ease the strain, especially since he had a tendency, since his illness, to become very emotional. I wanted this birthday party to be a happy time for him. Surprising Cliff with a puppy would be the best gift ever! I could hardly wait to see his reaction!

According to our plan, John had quietly brought the little puppy over earlier, placing him in the guest bedroom while Cliff was getting dressed in the bathroom. We hid the crate in the guest bedroom closet, keeping our fingers crossed that he would not make a sound. Once Cliff was dressed and downstairs, we were safe.

The music will drown out whatever sound this pup makes, I thought. John stayed upstairs in the guest bedroom with the puppy while I helped Cliff get dressed. When the coast was clear, he snuck out the front door. Living in a split-level home made it convenient to sneak around without being seen. I gave a sigh of relief.

Everyone arrived on time with gifts in hand and smiles on their faces. John returned with his wife and children. Everyone else had arrived with cheerful greetings. There would be no tears tonight. We had experienced enough sadness over the last few months to flood the ocean. Tonight, we would indulge ourselves eating cake, ice cream, and other comfort foods. And pray our time together would be remembered during the not-so-good times ahead.

After eating, it was time to open the gifts. Each person ceremoniously presented Cliff with a personal gift and a birthday hug. He was delighted, savoring every moment with a big grin. I could see him fighting back the tears. A bittersweetness filled the air, as everyone struggled to hold back tears leaking from their hearts. It was as if what was *not* spoken out loud was felt strongly in our souls: this could be the last time we celebrate a birthday with Cliff. Without saying a word, I rushed upstairs and returned just as quickly, supporting the little puppy's crate in my arms, beaming with pride.

I knew I had made the right decision to buy a puppy for Cliff's birthday when I saw the look on his face. He was ecstatic when he saw the little furry creature. It felt like something extraordinary that had been lost had just been found! The little puppy he visited so frequently on his walking trips at the mall now belonged to him!

I can't believe my eyes! It's Grand Master! I am a surprise for Grand Master, but it feels like Grand Master is a surprise for me! My tail is moving back and forth so fast, I'm afraid it's going to fall on the

floor. When Grand Master sees me, he opens his eyes wide, gets out of his chair, and grabs me out of my crate. (I thought he was going to squeeze me to an early grave.) Then everybody starts talking to the lady, calling her Lee.

"Lee, you really pulled a fast one!" Grand Master says smiling from ear to ear, and still holding me tight. "What's his name?"

"Coco! Let's name him Coco!" Lee shouts. "You know how much I love chocolate!"

"Coco Jordan," someone else yells. "Let's call him Coco Jordan." (Someone calls her Jean, saying she is a Michael Jordan fan.)

And what is a Michael Jordan? Must be something good! No one asks me about my name! Don't I get a say?

Like she knows what I'm thinking, the lady they call Jean says, "Coco Jordan, named after the greatest basketball player of all time, number forty-two!" Everyone laughs.

All by itself, my little tail begins wagging faster than usual. Coco Jordan is in the house!

LOOKING BACK

Watching the joy that Coco brought to Cliff's life was so gratifying. (The name Coco Jordan took too much time to say when we really wanted his attention, so we affectionately called him Coco.) During the days that followed his birthday party, Cliff had more energy. He took Coco every place he went. They were inseparable. The doubts that I initially had about Cliff being able to take care of a puppy had been eradicated. Feeding Coco treats was the delight of his day. Watching Coco garble those doggie cookies down always made Cliff laugh. He needed to laugh. *We* needed to laugh.

Seeing Cliff so happy, I couldn't help but reminisce about our life before it was shattered. The time spent together during the years that we dated and the early years of our marriage seemed so…natural. I never realized just how precious those times were until we began this journey of survival. We were healthy and happy then. We solved our problems together. And Cliff was so spontaneous. I remember clearly when, after only a few weeks of dating, he invited me to go with him to Hawaii on our next school break. I refused, feeling things were moving too fast, but opted to invite him to travel with me to my home in North Carolina for Christmas (if we were still dating by then) to meet my family. He insisted that we drive, explaining the long drive would give us some time to get to know more about each other. I agreed.

Cliff did all the driving, stopping along the way to give us time to sightsee, refresh, and get a bite to eat. Several times, I caught him adjusting his rearview mirror sideways to get a quick glance at me whenever he thought I wasn't looking his way. I was amused. The thirteen-hour drive seemed so much shorter than my usual trips home. This was the beginning of many more trips together.

After more than a four-year courtship, we decided to get married. Previously, we talked frequently about getting married, but we both had reservations when it came to setting a timeline. Growing up, I didn't have a lot of "happily ever after" role models to encourage me, and I was not even sure what it meant to be a good wife. Cliff had been married before we met, and the breakup had left its scars. Nonetheless, we finally decided to take the plunge and hoped that our love for each other would see us through any rough times. I considered Cliff being older than me to be an advantage. I was twenty-seven, and he was thirty-three at the time. I convinced myself that his wisdom and life experiences would compensate for my lack of knowledge about the world and my naïveté about marriage. Most of my married friends had already started their families. We could not afford to wait much longer.

From the beginning, our marriage presented us with some unexpected challenges, but none that we could not solve together. Regrettably, we innocently decided to build a new home before exchanging our vows with hopes it would be completed by our wedding day. We knew we wanted to buy a house, and we didn't see the value in paying money for an apartment when we could use that money toward paying off a mortgage. Made sense at the time.

Unfortunately, accumulating such a huge debt so early in our marriage proved not to be the best plan. Building a house presented some additional challenges, as we negotiated with the developers to get a move-in date before the wedding. The house was completed just in time. Amazing! Later, we discovered maintaining a home was never ending, even a new house. Our budget was always stretched too tight for comfort, which often led us to some very uncomfortable conversations about money.

Neither of us really knew what we were getting into—stacking the deck early on with a huge debt. Furthermore, I had my share of emotional baggage, stemming from my chaotic childhood, that I unpacked slowly and consistently on our journey of adjusting to the responsibilities of married life. I didn't have a lot of knowledge about budgeting and money management; growing up, we never had enough to manage. We lived paycheck to paycheck. That practice continued while out on my own. I made a decent salary at the time, but student loan payments and household expenses left little money for savings.

Cliff was raised in a big family in central Florida with his share of family stressors and emerged with some insecurities as well. A sickly child battling hay fever, he couldn't join the armed services after graduating high school like his older brothers and many other young Black men in his community. But with the encouragement of some of his teachers and his love for football, he decided to go to college—which turned out to be the best thing he could have done. Influenced by his godparents, who were both educators, he pursued a major in education. His teaching career eventually took him to upstate New York, where we met.

Cliff's father was deceased by the time we were married. Both parents were respected members of their church and church community and made sure their children attended church regularly. His mother was a strict disciplinarian who believed, like many parents, in using the rod for fear of spoiling the child. Cliff didn't talk much about their relationship, but I knew he loved her. He was a loyal son who treated her with the utmost respect.

Cliff enjoyed a close relationship with his siblings, especially his brothers. Whenever they were all together, even late in their adulthood, the room was filled with laughter, as they talked about sports, childhood pranks, and the many "whuppins" they received. Cliff was especially close to his youngest brother, James, who was actually living with him when we met. A tragic accident took his life a few years afterward. Cliff was never the same. A light in his life had gone dim.

Ironically, both Cliff and I were greatly influenced by our godparents. They inspired us to strive for academic excellence. We worked really hard to achieve it. We also needed the approval that they so willingly gave. Cliff and I knew we were blessed to have the support of such loving and giving guardians in our lives. We looked forward to their visits with us as well as our visits home with them.

As educators, we wanted to be good role models for our students in the same way our godparents were for us. We threw ourselves into our work, striving for perfection. Taking pride in being workaholics, we knew there was nothing more important than nurturing our students. Cliff was even more devoted, spending many hours after school and weekends with parent conferences and student activities, in and out of school. His classes were famous for taking educational field trips to exciting places: Washington, DC; Disney World; New York City; Niagara Falls; and more.

Summers were no different. Cliff usually taught summer school, and I worked as a director of a day camp for an agency in the community. Between buying a new house and paying off student loans, we needed the money. There were no complaints; we did what we had to do. When extra money *was* available, we rewarded ourselves for our hard work with much-needed vacations to someplace special. Whether it was enjoying the beauty of Maui or the Bahamas or spending time with family and friends across the country, we always felt renewed when we returned home.

Even though my biological clock was ticking, Cliff and I decided to wait a few more years—until the time was right—to have children. At that point, we could not afford children, money-wise or time-wise. As a nontenured educator, I wanted to get a few years under my belt before embarking on the unforeseen tasks of motherhood. I was also dealing with health issues that could possibly interfere with a pregnancy. As we waited for the right time to start a family, we continued updating our credentials to advance our careers. That time to start a family never came.

FROM CRATE TO KING
OF THE CASTLE

Life is good! Grand Master, Lee, and Coco Jordan—we're a family! We go almost everywhere together! Everyone tells me how cute I am everywhere we go. (Lee said my underbite made me look even more adorable in a strange sorta way.) Everyone we meet wants to play with my cute little furry ears—except Grand Master's friend, Joe, who comes by to see him all the time. I heard him tell Grand Master that I'm an ugly little thing. Grand Master looked at me. Rubbing my back, he said, "Joe's not a dog lover." I didn't care what Joe was! I get a lot of attention from everybody else, and I love it!

Grand Master is happy that I'm already potty trained. Doggy heaven knows they hounded me about it all the time at the pet store. "No one wants a dog who's not potty-trained!" These words landed like an annoying fly buzzing around my ears! I was out of my crate to do my business in no time.

Grand Master and Lee leave me out of my crate when they go out, and I'm always dry when they return. (Lee said, "No spots on the carpet!") I'm on a mission. I don't want to use those doggy diapers *she's going to buy for me if I have too many accidents. Lee even took me to the pet store just to show me what they looked like—in case I needed them! I make sure those doggy diapers never cross her mind. The good thing is, Lee and Grand Master never leave me alone for too long.*

Grand Master and Lee let me have the run of the house (feels like the king of the castle) as long as there are no accidents. Boy, am I careful! I like sliding across the kitchen floor while Grand Master or Lee chases me. I guess you know, they never catch me; I'm too fast! Sometimes Lee and Grand Master's friends come over and play with me. They try to catch me too. No way, José! I dodge here and there and everywhere. I'm gone before they can say, "Hot diggity dog!"

Bringing Coco Jordan home truly was the best gift ever! Cliff spent much of his time cuddling Coco and chasing that little pup all over the house. He was adorable. And he was growing all too fast. It had barely been six months since we brought him home, and his body had already changed so much. Coco was now starting to look like the Pekingese we saw on those televised dog shows. We always thought they were so cute—and tough! His silky, floor-length hair was a mixture of light brown, dark brown, and black colors that parted naturally down the center of his back and fell along both sides of his long and slender torso. Afraid Coco's hair would grow long enough to sweep the floor, we kept it nicely trimmed. And those short, stubby legs! I was always afraid he would tumble over. They didn't appear strong enough to support his strong, muscular body. Besides a rugged upper torso, Coco had an oversized head and furry ears that flopped on both sides of his face. Fluffy bangs covered his eyes, while short, black, and silky fur—extending from both sides of his nose—wrapped around his chin, providing a unique backdrop for the most lovable little facial features ever.

Coco's crown jewels were his precious, big, and beautiful dark-brown eyes that protruded slightly from their sockets just enough to mesmerize anyone. They even seemed to glow in dark hours of the night. Those bright eyes sat slightly above a cute little nose and looked like a piece of coal used to complete the face of a snowman. His nostrils were so tiny he often had trouble breathing, especially at night. Although Coco's adorable underbite was a unique characteristic of a Pekingese, his lower set of teeth missed a tooth in the center that had been pulled when Coco was only weeks old to alleviate overcrowding. If it weren't so, he would have made a great show dog.

What a face! But it was Coco's tail that demanded everyone's full attention. This big, bushy tail that waved like a flagpole in the early morning breeze consisted of a mixture of long and silky blond and dark-tan hair. I kept it neatly trimmed to make it easier for him to potty. The extraordinary feature of Coco's tail was its wag. I often referred to it as "the great communicator." When he was happy, this bright, bushy flag of a tail wagged relentlessly, like the blades of a cooling fan on a hot summer day.

When Coco was happy, everyone in his presence was happy. His playful mood, accented by the inevitable wagging of his tail, invited even the most cautious stranger to give him a pat on the head. On the other hand, there was nothing sadder than when Coco's tail drooped. The sight of his tail tucked between his legs tugged at my heart. I knew a droopy, tucked-in tail signaled fear, pain, doubt, or some other worrisome emotion. And I couldn't bear the thought of my little Coco suffering. I wanted his life to be as happy as the joy he had brought into our lives. Yes, Coco was our little prince!

My favorite thing to do is go for rides in Grand Master's big car. Lee's car is okay—just a little small for my liking. Too much like that cramped cage at the pet store. Lee drives, and I sit on Grand Master's right knee so I can push myself up on my hind legs to see out of the window. Sometimes, I see grass spotted with a lot of colors and tall trees. (Oh boy! I can have a good time marking those trees!)

When it's cold outside, everything turns white, and we don't go outside much. Lee's not much for driving on the white stuff. When we go out for a walk, the trails become shorter and shorter as the white stuff gets bigger and bigger. Sometimes, I get lost walking through it. Grand Master has to pull me out of deep holes. I come out shaking white stuff all over his rubber boots. (Not so sure he thinks that's as funny as I do.)

Mealtime makes me jump up and down! I can't stay still when I see food! Grand Master feeds me anything I want to eat. Lee doesn't like that! She read someplace that feeding a dog too much of what she calls "table food" can make him sick. (That must have been someone who never had a dog. What's the fun in living if you can't eat a good meal? I don't know of too many dogs who eat the dry stuff. I hear it tastes like cat litter…ugh!) Grand Master even drops a piece of cake or sweet bread from his plate when Lee's not looking. Sitting under the table where Lee and Grand Master eat is my favorite hangout. This table is so cool! You can see right through it! I never know when a treat will show up…yum, yum. Never want to miss a treat!

Coco was usually the first one awake, jumping on the bed and nudging one of us to take him out to do his business. I thought it strange that, on this particular morning, there was no Coco. But I decided to take advantage of staying in bed a little longer. That didn't happen too often, and I was not going to miss the opportunity to sleep in, especially since Cliff wasn't awake.

After a while, I got worried. *Where is Coco?* Cliff was still asleep. He must have had a rough night. Sometimes, when Cliff could not sleep at night, he slept later the next morning. I jumped out of bed and looked around for Coco. Approaching the hallway leading to the other bedroom, I saw Coco lying very still on the hallway floor. His eyes were glassy, and he was staring into space.

"Coco!" I yelled. He did not move. "Coco!" I yelled even louder.

"What's wrong with Coco?" Cliff yelled, jumping out of bed.

By the time Cliff got to the hallway, Coco was up on his feet. He shook his body a little and tried to walk. But he was unsteady. I knelt down and pulled him close to me.

"Are you okay, buddy?" I asked, rubbing his back and watching him carefully.

Cliff knelt down beside us and gently pulled Coco next to him. Coco rested his head on Cliff's leg looking dazed.

"I'll call the vet," I said, getting up from the floor. "Something's wrong."

The vet explained that Coco probably had a mild seizure. The diagnosis was confirmed when we took him in for treatment that afternoon. The vet assured us that Coco would be fine, but we needed to give him some medication to control the seizures. Hours after we returned home, Coco was running around like nothing had happened. Cliff and I, on the other hand, were still a bit shaken. We didn't want to admit how scared we were. But we could see it in each other's eyes. (The pet shop never mentioned that Coco had seizures.) We just couldn't lose another dog! Not Coco!

The good news was that the medicine was working. Coco had no trouble swallowing the pill, as long as we hid it in some peanut butter or a cheese ball, as the vet suggested. Sometimes, we treated him by hiding the pill in a meatball. Coco loved meatballs!

Cliff and I continued giving Coco all the love and attention he wanted. We were so thankful that he was such a good, and otherwise healthy, dog. He was forever romping around the house or the yard like the Energizer Bunny. He loved to play. His favorite toy was my bedroom slipper. When Coco was a young pup, we made the terrible mistake of tossing our slippers around for him to fetch and nibble on between throws. Cliff got such a kick out of seeing Coco dash for the slipper and corner it to keep us from taking it away from him. With my slipper tightly tucked between his teeth and his head swishing from side to side on a mission of destruction, he always enticed us to join the fun. We lived to regret the mistake we made when Coco began attacking the feet (shoes) of everyone who entered our home. Now, that was quite embarrassing! While I was awkwardly apologizing and trying to explain my dog's shoe fetish, my guests were usually busy taking off their shoes to be used as a toy. Coco had lured them into his playground.

I simply loved Coco's independent spirit. Many times, when I took him for a walk, he ran ahead of me, grabbing the end of the leash nearest his body. Clenching it between his teeth as tight as he could, Coco strutted with his fluffy tail pointed toward the sky and wagging with dignity, signaling, "I'm in charge here." This always prompted someone passing by to chuckle and comment that old expression, "Are you walking the dog, or is the dog walking you?" I usually just shook my head, smiled, and kept walking—with Coco in the lead.

That's the way it was with Coco. Everyone who met him wanted to be a part of his life or make him a part of theirs. He was always eager to oblige!

DANCING WITH DEATH

Grand Master and I go for long walks when he's not tired. The grass with lots of different colors is growing everywhere, and the white stuff is gone. I miss the white fluffy stuff. But not when I slip and slide on it. Almost broke a leg! The funny smells coming from the grass tickle my nose if I get too close. Sometimes Grand Master walks me so fast. Those are the good times. My little legs get really strong! Lee gets mad. She says I'm too young to walk so fast, but Grand Master knows I can keep up. Thing is, Lee always has to find a place to sit while we walk ahead. (Lee's not strong like Grand Master and me!)

Sometimes it's hard for Grand Master to keep up with me. I can tell when he's getting tired. He lets me get in front. (Man, I feel like a hotshot…Grand Master walking behind me!) I try not to walk too fast when he starts breathing funny. Lee would be so mad at me if I came home without him. I can't let that happen.

It had been more than a year since Cliff's birthday party. Cliff had been doing well, mainly due to having Coco around. Coco

kept him active. But I could feel it in my spirit. Things were
starting to change. Cliff was getting weaker and weaker by the
day. I think even Coco knew that something was wrong. Some
days, returning from a walk, Coco would be walking so far ahead
of Cliff. Whenever I walked out to meet them, Coco would stare
at me with those big, beautiful eyes, indicating something was
wrong. The time the doctors warned us about was finally coming: Cliff was entering the final stage of his illness.

Our world crumbled when faced with the reality that Cliff
had cancer. I remember it like it was yesterday. Cliff and I were
eating breakfast one Saturday morning. We were sitting on stools
at the breakfast bar in our newly renovated kitchen. Having lived
in the same house for almost twenty years, we were very excited
about our new kitchen. The portion of the wall we had removed,
which separated the dining room and the kitchen, gave us just
enough space for a small breakfast bar. We loved it and ate there
whenever we were able to eat breakfast together, which was mostly
on the weekends. This morning seemed no different from any
other Saturday morning. Our breakfast was simple: grits, eggs,
toast, bacon, and rice. I wanted grits. Cliff wanted rice. He hated
grits. (Sometimes, we treated ourselves by going out to breakfast.)

The bar was only big enough for two people to sit comfort-
ably. We always sat side by side, facing the formal dining room,
in order to see the morning news on a small television sitting
on the dining room table across from us. Cliff was addicted to
watching the morning news. He said it helped get his day off to
a good and informed start. As a teacher, he often quizzed his students to encourage them to keep up with world events. However,
this morning, the television had not been turned on as usual.
Puzzled, I quickly headed toward the television.

"I have cancer," Cliff blurted as if he had finally gotten the courage to say it out loud. The words pierced my ears like a bolt of lightning flashing across the sky. After a long pause, I heard myself scream…the scream turned into a wail…and finally, a groan.

"That's why it was so hard to tell you," Cliff responded with a crackle in his voice. "I knew you would do this," he continued as his voice strained. "I can't handle the tears—not today," he persisted, raising his voice a little.

Hearing those words and the hurt in Cliff's voice, I immediately became silent. It was as if someone had suddenly shut off the faucet: no drip, no drop. Cliff needed me to take the news like a man. I felt like I had been hit in the heart with a hammer, and he wanted me to *take it like a man*? Well, I couldn't take it like a man! I am not a man! I am a woman! And women don't take it like a man. We cry. We wail. We moan. We groan. Then, and only then, we come to our senses.

"Okay…I'm okay," I muttered, wiping my nose on the sleeve of my robe. I realized at that moment I was making things worse. I wasn't sensitive to what Cliff was going through. I was only thinking about myself: *my* hurt, *my* pain.

Convinced that I had calmed down, Cliff whispered, "The cancer is stage four."

I tightly clenched my jaw to keep myself from having another crying fit. *Stage four is a death sentence*, I thought.

"What kind is it?" I asked reluctantly, afraid of the answer.

"Non-Hodgkin's lymphoma."

"What are we going to do? What does the doctor say?" I responded, struggling to get the words out without tears. I didn't know much about this type of cancer, nor did I know anyone who had endured it.

"Well, the doctor is trying to get me into a clinical trial. There is a new medicine that they are trying out. It sounds hopeful."

My mind immediately fast-forwarded to thoughts of all the dreadful things I had heard about chemo: nausea, diarrhea, and hair loss. "How did this happen?" I asked in a strong voice, being careful not to upset Cliff more. "You get regular physicals; you work out all the time. What happened?"

There was silence—a very long and uncomfortable silence. It seemed neither one of us wanted to take the risk of speaking for fear of what the other's reaction would be.

"I don't want anyone to know about this," he finally responded, ignoring my questions. "I don't want people feeling sorry for me. I am going to beat this."

I was living through a nightmare. It all seemed so surreal. I was speechless. My heart ached. My stomach felt nauseous. I was lightheaded. But I had to keep it together for Cliff's sake. "Lord, help me," I whispered. "Help me, please!"

"I won't tell anyone." My lips moved robotically after another period of silence. "Will you tell your brother?"

"I don't know…" His voice trailed off. "We'll see."

There was something final about the way Cliff sounded. I wanted to pull him close and give him a big hug—I needed a hug, but I sensed he was doing everything he could do to be strong for both of us. We both knew we'd had enough excitement for one morning. I felt like I would faint if I didn't get some fresh air.

"I'm going up to take a shower," I said, gently brushing my hand across the back of his shoulder. Still, I hesitated to get up. I didn't know if my feet would steady me. My legs were limp, and my feet were numb.

I finally pulled myself up from the barstool, holding on to the arms of the stool for dear life. Thank God it had arms! My feet slipped away from the footrest on the barstool, and my toes reached for the floor. Luckily, my feet found a spot to anchor themselves. Miraculously, I stood up like a soldier called to attention by his superior. I stood still for a long time before attempting to move, hoping Cliff might give a sign he needed me to hold him. He didn't.

Then the strangest thing happened. I felt a warmth flow through me, like the sun was kissing every inch of my body. This warmth gave way to a sense of peace and calm I had not experienced since my mom passed—when God had rescued me from falling apart at the sight of her lifeless body nestled in her coffin at her viewing. I knew God had answered my prayer. He had come again and rescued me from serious trouble. My mind, body, and soul had been broken again. But God had not forsaken me.

I vaguely remembered seeing my husband walk toward the living room, located next to the kitchen, as I slowly lifted my feet up the short set of stairs, one step at a time, to get to the bathroom. Walking as if I were in a hypnotic state, I finally reached my destination. Stepping slowly into the shower, I turned the water on and cried uncontrollably.

What's going on here? Grand Master's not taking me for my walk? He looks tired a lot. Maybe he's still sleeping. He used to laugh a lot when I tugged at his slipper…no more. Lee walks me every day, but it's not the same. She's a slow walker. I need Grand Master—a

fast walker like me. Grand Master and Coco—we're a team. But he never lets me forget who's in charge. Grand Master says he's the master, but I'm the king!

Whenever Lee sits me down next to her on the couch, I know something's wrong. Lee never lets me on the couch. I see water rolling down the side of her face. Is she crying? Lee begins rubbing my ears like always when she wants to tell me something bad. Where is Grand Master? Why isn't he here to hear the bad news? Why do I have to hear it alone? I'm getting worried. I start barking nonstop until Lee rubs my back to calm me down. She always knows how to calm me down. We know when we need to help each other. That's the way it is with Lee and me.

Lee starts whispering in my ear, but I can't hear her. Did she forget how to talk? As I lift my ears up to try to hear what she is saying, I see she's crying. (Wow, this must be really bad!) I put my head on her lap and wait.

Lee tells me Grand Master is sick with something called cancer, and he won't be able to walk me anymore. Sounds bad! She says he will be sleeping most of the time. Lee wants me to be a good boy and not make a lot of noise. Grand Master needs his rest. (Whew! What a relief! I thought she was going to tell me they were taking me back to the pet store where they found me.)

Things aren't the same with Grand Master and this cancer thing. Lee is very sad all the time. Taking care of Grand Master is hard for her; she is tired all the time. She takes me for walks, short walks—not the long, fast walks Grand Master and I take. We don't play together like before. When Grand Master is awake, he lets me sit on his lap, and he rubs my head. I like that. He's too tired to play, but that's okay. I'm happy just sitting on his lap. Grand Master and Coco: the boys!

Now, Grand Master is sick with something Lee calls an infection. Not sure what that is, but it makes him feel bad and sleep a lot. Lee wakes up before the sun comes up to put one end of something she calls a tube, hanging from a bag of water, to another tube coming out of Grand Master's arm. Her eyes are red, and she looks like I look when I need a nap. I see her fingers moving a lot trying to get the tube in the right spot. Grand Master always goes to sleep when the water starts dripping though the tube. Poor Lee! She checks that tube over and over again before she goes to work. She must think that tube will disappear. My heart hurts thinking about it. I want to help her, but I'm just a dog. All I can do is put one paw over my eyes and lick the other one like crazy until my hurt goes away.

Lee talks to me a lot when Grand Master is sleeping. My ears are perked and ready to listen. I'm happy Lee never talks to me like I'm a young puppy. (No coochy coo talk in this house!) Lee talks to me like I'm smart. And she treats me like I'm special—except for that time I chewed a hole in one of her favorite socks. Oh boy, that was a dog of a different color!

I see why Lee wanted to give Grand Master a dog for his birthday. Everyone knows that Grand Master loves dogs. Lee says he had a lot of dogs in the house at the same time before me. When she met Grand Master, he had a dog named Princess. (What kind of name is that for a dog?) He loved Princess so much, and he took her everywhere (just like he did with me before that cancer got in the way). Lee let me smell her picture. What a beauty! She was small—not big like me. Her eyes look like a light, and her ears flop like my ears. She looks like quite the flirt! My tail curls just thinking about her. Enough of that!

Lee said she never took care of Grand Master's other dogs like she takes care of me. She didn't really like dogs so much...afraid they would bite her. (How could she think a dog would bite a nice lady like her?) She said dogs were not allowed in the house where she lived. They were yard dogs. Poor things! She said they ate table scraps and bones left in the yard for them. Where Lee lived, dogs were not a man's best friend. Don't know about that, but table scraps and bones sound mighty good to me...yum! All I get now is the dry stuff!

Lee changed her mind about dogs when she met Grand Master. She knew she had to like Princess. Grand Master and Princess were a team, like us. When Princess went to doggy heaven, a place Lee said dogs go if they have been good, Grand Master was sad for a long time. He said, "No more dogs."

Then, Grand Master got another dog! They called him Rusty. Rusty went to doggy heaven too. Lee said Rusty was a Chinese chow and a looker like me. Rusty got a lot of pats on the head when they took him for walks (like me). Grand Master had him a long time. Strange thing is, Rusty died of that cancer thing. And now Grand Master has cancer! If Grand Master didn't have cancer, I wouldn't be here. A human's life is confusing. Makes me happy to be a dog!

Being the primary caregiver for Cliff was a terrifying experience. I had zero knowledge about nursing skills. In fact, I shied away from hospitals, needles, and the sight of blood whenever I could. In-home care and help from family and friends were readily available, but as Cliff's wife, I was expected to take care of such routines as monitoring his medicines, changing any necessary bandages, cleaning his chemo port, and administering at-home IV's when necessary. I was desperate to do anything I could to help Cliff get better, but I was a nervous wreck. I agonized constantly about whether or not I had done the right thing, or if a procedure had been done properly. It would have been unbearable if something had gone wrong or if something I had not done compromised Cliff's health. By the grace of God, I was conscientious and did the best I could.

Our continued battle with cancer (such an appropriate term… *battle)* cultivated a life of solitude, especially in its late stage. Cliff, Coco, and I spent many hours alone. We couldn't do many of the things we used to do. Either Cliff was too weak, or I was too tired. We enjoyed visits from supportive friends and family members. Thank God for John and his family. One of them visited Cliff practically every day. However, much of our amusement centered on watching and helping Coco grow from a doting puppy to an independent alpha dog. All things considered, we still felt blessed!

When he was first diagnosed with cancer, Cliff was administered a series of chemo treatments. After several rounds, he was in remission. We were so relieved! Remission meant more time for researchers to find a medicine that worked to prolong life for people with this dreaded disease—maybe even a cure. But it was not sustainable. Remission only lasted less than a year. Then, it was back to more invasive treatments.

Cliff's doctor was successful in getting him into a clinical trial, but there was no long-lasting effect. Cliff was disappointed—even though we were warned about the odds—and started making plans to attend any and every conference he could find regarding new treatments for his type of cancer. He read articles about new treatments in Mexico and other countries, desperate to find a glimmer of hope.

Nonetheless, we began thinking about the future. Cliff was still determined to beat this thing. His sister, Clara, was given a death sentence because of cancer, and she lived twenty more years—long enough to see all her children grow up and establish lives of their own. Cliff felt encouraged.

"If Clara did it, I can do it!" he often reminded me.

We continued to plan for a future. First, we decided it was time to sell our present home and build another. Cliff's bout with cancer made us realize that we needed a home that would accommodate us in our retirement years: no stairs and handicap accessible. Cliff had already retired, and I had a few more years to go. We wanted to be better prepared for the next phase of his cancer or another illness that might sneak up on us.

In the past, Cliff and I had long conversations about moving south one day. He was born in Florida, and I was born and raised in North Carolina. We even talked about moving to California to be closer to one of his brothers and one of my sisters; yet, more than likely, we would be headed south. Cliff's cancer diagnosis had squashed all of those plans.

So, after the school year ended in mid-June, we put our house up for sale. Much to our surprise, two weeks later, we had a buyer. The buyer made a cash offer with the condition of moving in as soon as possible. We took the offer and made arrangements to move into a hotel room not far away. We had plans to stay at the hotel until we were able to move into our new home, which would be ready, we were told, in approximately four months. We put our furniture in storage, taking only the bare necessities with us to the hotel. The room had a microwave, a small refrigerator, and two queen beds, which gave us more room space. The hotel conveniently offered free breakfast every day and delivery services from nearby restaurants. It certainly was not ideal, but we were determined to make it work. After all, what choice did we have?

Our new home design had a ranch floor plan with no stairs and doorways wide enough to move a wheelchair in and out. Other amenities, such as better lighting, an alarm system, etc., were selected to make life easier if we were ever housebound due to an illness. And there was a large backyard for Coco to run and play. We had it all worked out.

Cliff was having a lot of good days. He was so excited about our new home and took an active part in supervising its construction, visiting the site every day. I was so happy that he had something to give him a purpose for the days ahead that distracted him from thinking about his cancer. Cliff still had moments and days when his body was tired and weak. But he kept fighting. We were planning for a brighter future. We even made plans to attend a conference in Texas where they were discussing new treatments at the MD Anderson Cancer Center (one of the best treatment centers for cancers like lymphoma). Cliff thought it might do us good to be able to talk with some of the expert researchers about our struggles finding an effective treatment. He had already booked flights for us. I wasn't so sure it was a good idea, but I was willing to give it a try. We had nothing to lose at this point. The conference was scheduled for a weekend in October, which gave us a couple months to plan for the trip.

Boxes are all over the house! Lee said it was time to move into a new home. I don't understand! I'm happy with this home. It's better than that cold cage they kept me in at the pet store. Why start all over again? Humans live a funny life! This new home is so much smaller—one room? Feels like my old cage. Where is my new cage,

the one Lee bought me when I waited to surprise Grand Master for his birthday? That was a big cage!

I didn't want to move to a new home...but it's fun to be in a small room with Grand Master and Lee. We're a team again—always together, except when Lee goes to work. Then it's just me and Grand Master! He lets me do anything I want to do and even feeds me table food! Love that ice cream...yummy, yum, yum! (I want the brown scoop, but he only gives me the white stuff. Said the other kind can make me sick.) Best part is, Grand Master lets me sleep in his bed. He puts me on the bed whenever he takes a nap. (Boy, he takes a lot of naps!) Lee said she didn't like me on the bed, but I'm sleeping with them all through the night—all the time! Can't get any better than this, I thought, until...it wasn't better.

The sun is so bright it hurts my eyes. Cliff and Lee are walking slower than before. I can feel it. Something isn't the same. I keep my nose to the ground and mark every tree in sight. Don't want them to see how worried I am. I can tell when something is going to happen. Grand Master and Lee—there's no talking and laughing a lot like before. Maybe they will tell me what's going on after my nap.

The sun is up, and I am ready to potty. Looks like a short walk. Lee is walking me fast. Whenever Lee walks me fast, it's a short walk. I'd better hurry and do my business. No time for circling for my spot. I knew it! She's already walking me back to the house! Something is wrong. I can tell. I'm ready for my grain bowl now. I'll worry about it after I eat.

I knew it! Grand Master and Lee tell me they have to go on a trip—without me. They say they won't be gone long and will come back to take me home. Then, they take me for another fast walk. After I finish my business, Lee puts me in the car and drops me off at some place called Puppy Paradise, with two nice ladies who call each other sister. They look don't look like the pretty lady who gave me cookies at the pet store. And they smell funny…like cat litter! The sisters say they will take good care of me while Grand Master and Lee are away. Maybe they'll give me all the treats I want to keep me happy! Just don't make me play with those other dogs!

The trip to Texas was a disaster. Cliff was not well enough to travel, but he insisted he was going on this trip. I had planned to meet him at the airport after dropping Coco off at our favorite kennel, Puppy Paradise. Coco was reluctant to stay, but he finally settled down. I assured him we would be back soon to take him home.

When I spotted Cliff sitting in the waiting area in the airport lobby, I wanted to cry. He looked so tired and could hardly hold his head up. I practically begged him not to go on this trip.

"You can't do this! You're too sick," I pleaded.

"I'm going," he insisted.

"Jean and I can go and take all the notes you need. I can get John to stay with you until we get back." My friend Jean had offered to travel with us in case I needed help with Cliff. She didn't want me to be alone in case of an emergency. I wish I had taken her offer.

Cliff was silent but determined to attend the conference. Finally, I relented and sat down next to him, hoping he would have a change of heart if I were quiet. He didn't. I just didn't feel right about Cliff going on this trip. But what could I do? He was adamant. It was a life-or-death mission for him. "Please, God, help us!" I prayed.

Fortunately, we made it through the conference. It was startling to see some of the attendees in their hospital beds, in wheelchairs, and walking with canes. They were just as determined to get to this conference as Cliff, hoping for a miracle cure. New treatments and therapies were discussed, but many of them were being investigated in clinical trials that would last for years. He did not appear to be a good candidate for any of them. Cliff did not seem to mind that we were leaving the conference early, having received little or no information of immediate help to us.

The flight back was horrendous! Cliff became so weak that I had to literally hold him up on his feet to get through the terminal to board the plane. I reserved a wheelchair for landing, but Cliff didn't want to use it. When he could no longer stand, he relented. The look on his face almost broke my heart. He was such a proud man. Using a wheelchair—in public, no doubt—almost destroyed him.

I was so thankful we were able to make it back to the hotel room without Cliff getting any sicker. So was he. He realized how sick he was. After helping Cliff get settled in bed, I retreated to the bathroom, covered my mouth with my hands, and let out a silent cry.

When I crawled into bed, Cliff was asleep. I felt relieved and whispered a prayer, thanking God for allowing us to make it home safely. I closed my eyes and drifted off to sleep. What seemed like a few hours later, Cliff was tossing and turning and moaning. He was in great pain. His forehead was hot, and he complained he was cold. Not taking any chances, I immediately called 911.

A TIME TO MOURN

Seems like Grand Master and Lee have been gone for a long time. They said they'd be back to take me home. Maybe they don't want me anymore. What did I do wrong? Did I walk Grand Master too fast when he was tired? Or maybe Lee was tired of me sleeping in her bed. Maybe the new house was ready, and they decided to move in without me. The sisters are nice to me, but I want to see Grand Master and Lee one more time. I want them to know I'm a good boy—no begging for table food or sliding on their pretty new floors!

I can feel it. Grand Master and Lee left me. I'm getting sick to my stomach thinking about it. Why did they leave me? I can't believe they left me there for so long. Will I see them again? The sisters play with me and feed me every day. But this is not my home. The sisters are not my family. There are too many dogs coming in and out. It's hard to make friends. Well, there's this cute little dog that looks like the picture I saw of Princess, living in the cage next to me. We hit it off just great. She's not a barker like the other dogs. I take a nap, wake up, and she's gone! I guess her mommy took her home. I'm getting lonely again. I want to go home too.

I sleep a lot, but I'm starting to play again. I have to go on. I can't let one bad break stop me from living. I'll be a good boy, and a nice family out there will soon take me home with them like Lee did. I miss Lee and Grand Master.

Still waiting. Not one new family has come by to even take a look at me! That's not the way it was at the pet store. I had people coming by my cage all the time. That's where I met Grand Master. My stomach feels sick again. I watch the sun come up and go down so many times that I know I won't get a new home. I guess the sisters are stuck with me. I try not to think about Lee and Grand Master, but watching the other dogs play makes me think of when we were together. So I nap. Whenever I close my eyes, I see myself running free in a field. I forget all about Lee and Grand Master.

Opening my eyes and stretching my body, I look around for that little pup I saw in the field. Don't see the little pup, but the sisters are coming my way with big smiles. Someone is behind them, but I can't see who it is. Looks like…Lee! Lee! She's here to take me home! I'm one happy fellow! Where is Grand Master? Maybe he's too tired to come in and is waiting for us in the car.

Lee picks me up and hugs me so tight that I can't breathe. I don't care! I missed Lee and Grand Master. I'm going home. Life will be good again! I let her squeeze me as long as she wants to squeeze me. We are together again! I can't wait to get to the car to see Grand Master. Lee thanks the nice sisters for taking care of me. She's still hugging me when we leave to go to the car.

I can tell that something's going on. Lee's not the same. Her face looks droopy, with no smile like before, and her eyes look wet. She looks like she needs a nap. When Lee opens the car door, there's…no Grand Master! Guess he's home taking a nap. Poor Grand Master. This cancer thing is so hard on him.

I was silent for a moment, afraid Coco had forgotten about us. He had been in the kennel for so long—almost two months. When he saw me, his whole body started wiggling as he darted toward me. Relieved, I scooped him up in my arms and hugged him for dear life. I could feel him hugging back. Walking toward the car with Coco still in my arms, I could see him searching for Cliff. When we got to the car, Coco's eyes hunted all over. He even stuck his head out the window to look around. Getting him settled, I rubbed him behind his ears and whispered, "Grand Master has gone to that place where humans go if they are good and can't get well."

It seemed like decades since I dropped Coco off at Puppy Paradise on our way to Texas. After the trip to Texas, Cliff got seriously ill. He was in so much pain that the doctors had trouble finding the right medication for him. They had given him all of the usual medicines for cancer pain, but nothing helped. Cliff's pain was so intense that he screamed out in agony for some relief. I felt helpless and scared.

Apparently, Cliff had an infection, which was common for cancer patients. However, the pain associated with the infection was out of control. He'd probably gone too long without treatment. I knew that trip to Texas was a bad idea. Why didn't I try harder to stop it? The guilt was tearing me apart. Now, we were faced with the dilemma of how much medication to administer for pain without causing more damage to Cliff's organs. In the end, a gradual increase in Cliff's pain medication to make him comfortable led to the inevitable. Cliff slept most of the time and became so weak he was totally bedridden. As the days and weeks passed, Cliff's condition worsened. During the nearly six weeks of his hospital stay, the doctors prescribed a number of treatments, but treating one thing led to a problem with something else. Finally, after days of being on a ventilator, Cliff transitioned November 19, 1999.

I'm really sad Grand Master couldn't get well. I hope he was good enough to go to that place where humans go if they are good—that place humans go if they are bad sounds really bad! Lee says we will have to get along without him. I miss Grand Master, but I'm happy to see Lee—happy she came back to get me. My little tail can't stop wagging. She says she will feed me, take me for long walks, and give me all the love I need. Just the two of us! I scoot my body over to her as close as I can and put my head on her lap. It's me and Lee now. Lee's quiet for a long time. Now I know why Lee looked so sad when she picked me up from the nice sisters. I put my paws over my eyes to hide the hurt.

Hold on! (My eyes open wide and my head pops up.) Grand Master won't be here to help me when we go for a ride! I will have to hold myself up to the window to see the cars and the flashing lights passing by all by myself! Lee sees the look on my face and begins rubbing my head and the back of my ears in just the right spot.

"Time to go home," she said.

Where are we going? Something's not the same! Lee tells me we have a new home. She says our new home has lots of room to run and play, even a big backyard with big trees. (Oh, how I love trees!) Maybe some doggy friends to play with. I don't care about the new doggy friends, but hearing about the trees make my tail wag. What a relief to be able to mark my own potty spots again!

Why is Lee so sad when we get to our new home? She leaves me in the car and goes in without me. I wait, and I wait. When Lee comes back, she takes me out of the car and presses my face to her face before she puts my feet on the ground. As she fastens my leash to the collar around my neck, she pulls me around to the backyard. Guess Lee knows I have to take care of a little doggy business first. We walk to the door, and Lee picks me up again and hugs me close to her chest. We go into our new home...together.

Cliff was gone. It was like a nightmare. His battle with cancer was finally over. He left us to mourn his death: a grieving widow and his precious dog, Coco. My life had been turned upside down. The sorrow was so heavy I could hardly breathe, especially at night. Nighttime was the worst.

Cliff and I had made his funeral arrangements while he was in remission. He was determined to get everything in order for whenever that final day came. Cliff selected his coffin and burial site and even wrote out the details for two home-going celebrations (a common reference for funerals in the Black community): one in New York and one in Florida. He had many family members living in his native hometown in Florida, some of whom were unable to travel to upstate New York to say their goodbyes. Cliff also wanted to be laid to rest in Florida in the family plot. So it made sense to have a service in Florida as well. However, attending two funerals had taken its toll on me. My dear sister was right by my side. I could not have survived these events without Joyce's support and presence.

I knew it would be hard getting back on my feet, but I underestimated the deep, dark loneliness that plagued me every day. Joyce had returned home. (She finally gave up trying to persuade me to go back home with her.) I was a year and seven months older than Joyce, though, at times, she seemed more mature. My world always felt more secure when she was around. She had a heart of gold; yet Joyce could be a pit bull if necessary. I missed her terribly, but I found comfort in knowing that I still had Coco. I needed him as much as he needed me. He missed Cliff too.

When we enter the house, Lee walks toward a room with a bed. Still holding me, she sits down on the floor in a corner near a window. Lee looks at the bed in the room so long that my little legs are getting tired of her holding me this way. Is she losing it? Water slides down her cheeks as she pulls me closer to her. I put my head on her shoulder. We are quiet for a long time in the dark. When I start to wiggle, Lee stands up and pulls something from the closet that looks like my bed but much bigger. She puts this big doggy bed next to her bed and covers it with a blanket. Lee sits down on it and calls me over to her. We curl up like two puppies trying to keep warm. This time, Lee closes her eyes for a long time. But I'm confused. Is Lee sleeping in my bed tonight? I get tired of watching her, so I close my eyes too.

I wake up with the sun shining in my eyes, but I don't see Lee. I hear noise in another room. Stretching my body as I walk to check things out, I see Lee sitting at a table looking out of the window. I look around for my morning meal. Where is my bowl? My favorite toy slipper Grand Master gave me? Everything is gone! I wish Grand Master were here. He could help me! All I could do was bark until Lee took me out to potty.

Lee plays with me all the time, but her eyes don't shine like before. They are wet all the time. Sometimes water comes down from her eyes and slides down the side of her face. I do all I can to comfort her. I snuggle and lick and wag until my tail is sore! I try to make Lee feel better, but I'm just a dog! When I see her looking too long, not blinking her eyes, I pull her nightgown (she wears her nightgown a lot) like I need to potty. She blinks her eyes, puts my leash on, and lets me out the side door to take care of my business. Sometimes I do, and sometimes I just smell around until Lee calls me in. Never knew not having Grand Master around would be so bad.

Many nights, I wished I had gone home with my Joyce. Living alone was tough—much tougher than I imagined. I couldn't stop crying. I often snuggled on the floor with Coco before bedtime hoping to fall asleep. Sleep would not come. My mind couldn't stop rehashing the many experiences Cliff and I shared: the good and the bad. I agonized over all the things I should have done when Cliff was alive. Reminiscing about all that had been lost made me even more sad. I felt Cliff's life had been cut short—at age fifty-seven—before he had the chance to fulfill all of his dreams. We both had planned to retire as soon as financially possible and move south, away from the brutal cold weather of upstate New York. (Cliff was forced to retire earlier due to the cancer.) We wanted to travel and visit with family living on the West Coast. It was not to be.

I felt so much guilt. Maybe I hadn't done all I could do to help Cliff find a treatment. I discouraged him from traveling to Mexico for an alternative approach. Was I wrong? It wasn't safe. My mind even went back to the one place I was determined not to go—the time Cliff and I almost got a divorce. Almost four years before we found out about the cancer, we were separated for a year. (We had been married for ten years prior.) I had literally moved back home to North Carolina at the end of the school year without knowing when or if I would return. Our relationship had crumbled under the stresses of working too hard and not being able to communicate clearly and effectively about our needs and desires. We argued a lot, unable to genuinely listen to each other. Cliff started working too much to avoid being home (or so I suspected), and I spent a great deal of time alone or with my girlfriends. We were putting all of our energy into our professions, leaving none for our personal lives—our marriage. We knew we were sinking, but we were unable or possibly unwilling to reach out to each other. It seemed whenever I did allow my vulnerability to show, Cliff was unable to respond in an emotionally helpful way, which pushed me away even further. It was the same for him. Trust was eroding, and our desire to be with each other was fading. I knew he was hurting. So was I. But I didn't have a clue about how to make things better. Apparently, neither did he.

I suggested we get professional help, but Cliff refused. He could not see how some outsider could help us solve our problems. Such a common male view, I thought. Counseling was our only hope of breaking this cycle of brokenness. In my profession as a school counselor, I frequently encouraged people to seek help. I was trying to do the same for us. Finally, I decided to get counseling alone to process my pain and explore my options. I didn't want a divorce, but I felt Cliff had given up on our marriage. It had died, and I couldn't bring it back to life on my own.

After too many nights of praying for the right answers, I thought God had turned away from me, displeased that I was considering breaking my marriage vows. A fog of guilt blurred my vision and distorted my view. I was lost and struggled to find a path forward. I was ashamed that I didn't have the necessary skills to save my marriage. After all, I was a trained professional. How is it that I could help other people salvage their relationships but not my own. I felt like a failure.

One night when I thought I would lose my mind, God intervened and spoke to my spirit. I was embraced by a sense of peace and calm that reminded me of God's love and His power over my life. He would not forsake me. His forgiveness would restore my soul. It became very clear to me that I needed to get away for a while. So I made plans to go home temporarily to clear my head and give Cliff and me some time to think things through without the noise of silence and confusion. Coincidentally, my godmother was having serious health issues. Going back home would allow me more quality time to assist in caring for her (rather than running back and forth), while taking the time I needed to determine the fate of my marriage.

Cliff wasn't happy about my leaving. He couldn't see how we could work things out apart. Nevertheless, I was convinced that being away from each other would give us a different perspective from which to negotiate our problems. Trying to resolve our disagreements in a positive way hadn't worked before; I wasn't expecting anything different at this point. I proceeded with my plans and prayed that the distance would create a space for clarity and reflection.

Sadly, most of our long-distance phone calls ended with both of us feeling exhausted, disappointed, and more hurt. After agreeing not to communicate with each other for a while, I received a long letter from Cliff filled with regrets, explanations, and a desire for reconciliation. Further, Cliff shared that he was getting counseling to guide him through this process. He wanted me to join him. Convinced after numerous phone conversations that he was serious about reviving our marriage, I flew to New York at Cliff's request, to meet with him and his counselor. I even consulted with Cliff's counselor before making a decision to meet. This was a huge step in the right direction, and I wanted to do my part. Besides, I never wanted a divorce: I wanted to be heard and seen in a healthy, thriving marriage. We were both hopeful that we could forgive each other and do the work necessary to put our marriage back on track. I knew we needed help to do so. This was our opportunity.

Cliff and I made frequent trips back and forth from North Carolina to New York to see each other until we were both comfortable enough to give each other and our marriage a second chance. I believed we deserved such. Unfortunately, three years after moving back to upstate New York and settling in for a new chapter in our relationship, Cliff and I were faced with the fiercest challenge and greatest threat of all: cancer.

All those months wasted being apart! The hurt and pain we caused each other! It didn't seem fair at first. In the face of cancer, the problems in our marriage seemed trivial at best. But God, in His most infinite wisdom, knew that I needed time away to be able to be in a space of grace and mercy to fulfill my marriage vows: for better, for worse, in sickness and in health, till death do us part.

Lee's getting better, but sometimes I hear her talking to someone. When I look up, no one is in the room but Lee and me. She talks to someone whenever she closes her eyes, but I never see who it is. It happens a lot after our bedtime routine—Lee yells, "Lord, help me!" One time, I almost fell off her bed trying to see who she was talking to. I didn't see anyone! Lee knew she had scared me. She started rubbing my back with her soft hands. (I love it when she rubs my back.) Water rolled down the side of her face as she pulled the blanket up close to her chin and closed her eyes. Now, whenever I hear her cry, "Lord!" I don't move! I know Lee talks to someone she calls Holy Spirit. She said it makes her feel better. But Lord is news to me. Makes me think she has a new man in her life. What do I know? I'm just a dog!

After a few weeks of being back home, I finally decided to visit Joyce. She had been begging me to come to California for a while, but I thought I was going to be okay. She had already spent so much time with me; I wanted her to have a break. Besides, I had not expected to have such a difficult time coping with Cliff's death and the loneliness. I was so grateful that I had Coco, but the grief was too raw. I felt like I was drowning. The thoughts of Cliff's illness and memories of the good times cut short were too much for me to bear. Going to California sounded like a great idea. This would be Coco's first plane ride. I was a little hesitant, but I couldn't leave him behind again. It was too soon. I thought it would be nice to get away from the cold weather for a while. So off to sunny California we went!

Only a few days after arriving in California, we got a call from my younger sister's daughter that my sister Faye, who lived in Connecticut, was seriously ill. Joyce and I were in shock! We had no idea Faye was so ill. We knew she had some health issues, but not this! I had to keep myself from falling apart, but this was almost unbearable. Cliff and now Faye? I was so glad that I was with Joyce and did not have to travel to Connecticut alone. Joyce, Coco, and I flew to Connecticut as soon as we could make flight arrangements.

Faye was in critical condition, but the doctors were hoping for the best. She seemed to be doing better by the time we decided to go back to our respective homes. Shortly after arriving back home, we were notified that Faye had taken a turn for the worse. The doctors were not optimistic. Sadly, Faye died a few days upon our return. We were all devastated.

Joyce and I visited with our niece for a few days following Faye's funeral and headed back home. Our lives were shattered. I didn't know how or if I could survive the pain and sorrow consuming me. The weight was traumatizing. I didn't want to go home where the memories of death would greet me at my door, but I needed to be with Coco. I had left him with his vet, promising to be back soon. Poor Coco! He had to think I was the worst mommy ever. I had to see him and hug him and let him know how much I needed him.

Lee told me her sister went to that place humans go if they are good. How much can a human take? Lee needs me now more than ever. Maybe I could help if I were human. But I'm just a dog. Grand Master…now her sister? I feel my eyes getting wet. I hate it when Lee pulls the blanket over her head at bedtime. I know it's coming when I see her wet face as she picks me up and puts me at the foot of the bed. I don't like those times, so I ease my way to her pillow and give her a nosey. When my nose touches her wet cheek, she looks at me and smiles. I like making Lee smile. Lee needs something to make her smile.

Lee loves playing a game she calls journal writing. I don't like that game. She won't let me play with her. "This is not a game for dogs," she said. Lee plays this game a lot for a long time. She even plays when the sun comes up before getting out of bed. When she stops playing the journal game, Lee plays some sleepy-time music. I'm always ready for a nap when I hear it. Lee gets up and moves around the room like she's free, wagging the end of her nightgown as she moves around the room. Sometimes I grab the other end of that nightgown and pull it so hard it makes Lee laugh. I love making Lee laugh. I hope Lee feels better when she laughs.

CHILDHOOD MEMORIES

Days passed slowly, and I was feeling sorry for myself. I needed Jesus, but I couldn't feel His presence. It was even hard to pray. The light inside of me had gone dark. I couldn't stop thinking about all those times in my life I felt alone and unloved. Living by myself triggered sad memories of the past when, as a child, I struggled to find my way in a life filled with chaos and confusion. Like Cliff, I grew up in a very large family: brothers, sisters, cousins, maternal grandmother and grandfather, aunts, and uncles. Many of us, at various times, lived together or in close proximity. My family—which was highly dysfunctional—exhibited a mishmash of personalities, behaviors, moods, and attitudes that kept our household in turmoil. Some family members abused alcohol, igniting an even more unstable environment for the children in the household. I still have vivid memories of sibling rivalry among adults in the family erupting into arguments because someone was inebriated.

Struggling to figure out where I belonged in this maze, I never found my place. According to my mom, Christine, affectionately called Ma, I was a very sensitive child who cried "at the drop of a hat." Expressing raw emotions, especially pain, was looked upon as a sign of weakness. Too many times, I felt trapped in my own feelings: my fears, uncertainties, and insecurities.

Ma was a gentle soul who was overwhelmed by the responsibilities of being a single parent who happened to be poor. In the late fifties, it wasn't easy for young Black mothers, especially those who were poor and uneducated, to earn enough money at primarily domestic jobs to take care of their families. It often took a village of family and friends to provide assistance—food, shelter, and resources, if necessary.

My siblings and I spent much of our early childhood living with our maternal grandmother and grandfather: Grandma and Papa. They worked the farms and demanded their children do the same in spite of their need for an education. They insisted everyone in the family work to help make ends meet. Ma worked long hours looping tobacco, picking cotton, cleaning houses, or washing dishes at local eateries—anything she could find to feed and house her children. But when work was not available, she relied on Grandma and Papa to help take care of us. It was not unusual for Grandma to surround herself with her daughters and their children, allowing them to live under her roof until they could get their lives together, which often meant finding a job. I recall a period of time when there were more than ten people living under one roof. We all lived in a house that we appropriately referred to as "the big house": Ma, her five kids, her two sisters, their kids, Grandma, and Papa. Looking back, I don't know how we managed.

During that time, Ma worked as a waitress and dishwasher at a cafe located across the railroad tracks—in the White section of town. Oftentimes, she would take one of us to work with her or arrange for us to visit her while at work. We loved going to the cafe. The owner was a very nice Jewish lady who was very fond of Ma. She served us hot dogs and doughnuts while we hung out in the kitchen and pretended to help Ma with the dishes. Spending time with her like that made me feel connected as a family. Being with Ma at the cafe was one of the few times I felt that way.

Growing up in a large, chaotic family, I felt invisible. I often indulged myself watching old movies on our black-and-white television (whenever no one else was watching), escaping into a world of romance and make-believe. I developed a love for reading and writing, which motivated me to do well in school: my safe space. I enjoyed the praise and recognition received from my teachers and classmates, and I spent many hours visiting my girl-friends, who seemingly had healthy, mostly middle-class homes. Their parents treated me like a member of the family. Practically living in their homes, especially on the weekends, I discovered they also had family problems that were not so visible, as did most families living in the segregated South.

Despite the turmoil, I recalled happy times while living in the big house, particularly during the Christmas season—my favorite time of year. A new pair of skates and a brown paper bag filled with an apple; an orange; red, green, and white Christmas candies; and nuts were all we wanted—and all our parents could afford.

Neighborhood kids skating together on Christmas morning, at a place we referred to as *the hill,* was one of my favorite childhood memories. The hill was a long, slightly inclined street that stretched from one end of a main road in our small hometown to another on the other side of town. This street was our gathering spot. On Christmas morning, after the neighborhood kids had opened their gifts, the older kids would come with their skates in hand, ready for a fun time.

We were always eager to see who the great skaters were: the ones who were crisscrossing and skating backward. On many occasions, a race would ensue. Those of us who were mediocre skaters would quickly get out of the way while the more skillful skaters dominated the road. We skated until late in the evening or until someone's mother or father (or aunt or uncle) yelled, "Streetlights are coming on. Time for y'all to be in the house." Instantly, the street emptied.

My life changed dramatically when I was in fifth grade. Prior to that, one of the teachers in my elementary school, whom I later referred to as my godmother (my fairy godmother), had taken me under her wing. Her name was Mrs. McDaniel. Mrs. McDaniel saw my potential and always encouraged me to do my best. She was aware of my family history and knew of our limited resources. She had also taught several children in our family. Although Mrs. McDaniel had a son a few years younger than me, she was well known for reaching out to numerous children in the school and the community who needed support to reach their potential.

At the end of the school day, I frequently visited her class-room to help her with classroom tasks: erasing the chalkboard, decorating a bulletin board, organizing papers—anything to be around her. Eventually, Mrs. McDaniel got permission from Ma for me to spend time at her house helping her with household chores: cleaning, washing, dusting, ironing, etc. She would pay me. Ma, knowing that her resources were limited, always wanted the best for us and was willing to accept assistance when offered.

A few hours a week doing chores at Mrs. McDaniel's house turned into overnight stays on weekends. By the time I reached fifth grade, I was virtually living with her full time. As my fifth-grade teacher, she became fully invested in my upbringing: nurturing me and providing me with whatever I needed to thrive. Other teachers also saw my potential and were instrumental in inspiring and motivating me to excel. Consequently, I graduated with the highest grade point average in my class and became the first member in our family to go to college. This support demonstrated the power and importance of the village in raising a child during this era.

It was evident Ma had a serious drinking problem and was finding it difficult to stay in one place. During my childhood, we knew very little, if anything, about alcoholism: that it was a disease like any other health condition that needed treatment. Instead, drinking excessively was a stigma and looked upon by some with contempt. Though it was often done secretly, drinking was common in most households where we lived. Truthfully, many people in our community drank to cope with the ills of segregation and poverty surrounding the Black communities.

I was terrified when Ma drank. Although she mostly indulged on weekends, especially when she was employed, her behavior changed drastically while under the influence: a quiet, soft-spoken, and gentle woman was transformed into an unpredictable, testy stranger. With one drink, Ma could face any demon that got in her way. My siblings and I worried constantly about her safety. We knew she was not as tough as she behaved while under the influence of alcohol.

Ma and Grandma did not get along most of the time, partly due to Ma's attitude when she drank and Grandma's favoritism toward some of the other siblings and their children. Ma was argumentative and rebellious when she had too much to drink, which often created conflicts in the family. Finally, Grandma demanded that Ma find a place of her own. Since she was between jobs at that time, we children lived separately with friends of the family and relatives until Ma could land a job that paid enough for her to get a place big enough for all of us. In my case, that never happened. I lived for a short time with my cousin, Dina, who lived near Mrs. McDaniel. Soon I began spending so much time at Mrs. McDaniels's house that she invited me to live with her for as long as I wanted. Ma agreed.

For many years, I agonized over why my mom would give me away, even though taking care of other people's children was common practice in our neighborhood. As I matured and, as a school counselor, began to counsel children from troubled homes, I realized what an unselfish act it was: making sure I was nurtured and supported, by any means necessary. I now understand Ma's sacrifice as her way of making sure I was taken care of, and fundamentally, an act of divine intervention.

At the age of ten, I began experiencing a completely different lifestyle while living with Mrs. McDaniel and affectionately began referring to her as my godmother. I no longer had to worry about food, clothing, or a safe place to live. While living with my godmother, I attended church regularly for the first time, participated in church-sponsored summer camps, and eventually sang in the church choir. The lyrics of so many of the songs we sang at church camp and in the church choir became my spiritual lifeline. I didn't understand it at the time, but words like "I need thee every hour"; "Precious Lord, take my hand"; "Jesus loves me, this I know"; and "Please don't pass me by" had been imprinted on my heart to comfort and strengthen me for years to come. In church school, I learned about the power of

God and why it was important to do the right thing in the eyes of God. These teachings became the foundation of my faith and my desire to be a *good* girl and to have a right relationship with God. They were essential to my spiritual growth.

After facing a multitude of problems trying to survive, Ma decided to relocate to a small town in Connecticut to get a new start. Aunt Viola, Ma's sister, who had already settled there, assured Ma she could make a better life for herself and her kids by moving up North. Up North was viewed as the land of opportunity by those of us who lived down South. Jobs were more plentiful, and White people were nicer, so we were told. Jim Crow laws enforcing racial segregation were not prevalent up North. (Jim Crow was a disparaging term for African Americans.)

Ma was grieving the loss of a very unhealthy romance at the time. It was the perfect time for her to try to begin a new life. I was a senior in high school and planning to go away to college. I was delighted that Ma had decided to live with Aunt Viola until she could get settled. I knew Aunt Viola would take good care of her. She was always so caring toward us and treated us like her own children.

Ma and Aunt Viola had married good friends, one of whom was my dad, when they were younger. Ma was only nineteen; Aunt Viola was a bit older. Ma's marriage to my dad lasted only a short while. I was a few months old when they separated and ultimately divorced. Aunt Viola was still married at the time. She was very protective of my mom and wanted to help her and us kids in any way she could. I loved her for loving us.

Ma did not seem to mind that I wanted to stay with my godmother to complete my senior year, instead of moving to Connecticut with her. Although I was happy to finally have the comfort of a secure and loving home, I still longed for a traditional family: a mom, a dad, sisters, and brothers, all living together under one roof, just like the White families I watched on television. Being separated from my biological family left me with a sense of abandonment—a feeling that resurfaced with Cliff's death.

Poor Lee! Grand Master leaving us is making her so sad. She still wipes her eyes a lot at night during our bedtime routine. And she makes sad sounds in bed like she's hurt. I want to help her, but I'm only a dog! I can help a dog stop hurting by giving him a big, yummy bone. But humans? Lee said not having Grand Master here makes her think of when her mom went to that place where humans go if they are good—before Grand Master went there. She was sad then like she's sad now. Hearing Lee's so sad, I put my paws over my eyes. I can't let her see my eyes get wet. Don't want her to get sad about me too!

Cliff's passing triggered enormous feelings of grief and loss not felt since the death of my mom. I was a bit surprised since I knew his life was ending. When my mom died in September 1973, two years before Cliff and I married, I thought my heart would never heal. It was so tragic. Joyce and I were sharing an apartment in upstate New York. I had recently completed my MA degree and was job hunting. Joyce had graduated college and decided to join me in New York to look for a teaching job.

We were so happy to finally be together again, in the same house. Fortunately, we were both able to find employment. I was hired as a school counselor—the first Black school counselor in that suburban school district—and Joyce was hired to teach elementary school children at a school in the city.

Returning home from a busy day at work, we were both tired and hungry. Instead of going out to eat, we decided to call Ma to get the recipe for her mouth-watering barbecue chicken. We knew barbecue chicken was not a quick and easy meal for two hungry working ladies who were not fond of cooking, but we had this incredible craving for Ma's delicious dish.

I picked up the phone and quickly dialed her number. I had a strange sense that something was wrong when Aunt Viola, not my mom, answered the phone. She recognized my voice.

"Chris is gone," Aunt Viola responded with such sadness.

Hearing the news, I bellowed a blood-curdling sound that I'm sure could be heard throughout my apartment building. Joyce immediately grabbed the phone. After a few seconds, with the phone to her ear, she let out a scream of her own. Ma had died from an assault by an ex-boyfriend—the one she relocated to get away from, but he had followed her to Connecticut. He had been stalking her. The authorities called it a crime of passion. The events that followed were blurred: traveling to Connecticut, planning and attending the funeral, returning to New York. I was devastated.

After Ma's funeral and a few weeks of rest, I returned to work. Joyce decided to stay in Connecticut to care for our younger brother, who was only six at the time and whose dad was the ex-boyfriend who killed our mom. Joyce and I had been so excited to finally get the chance to live in the same house at the same time. Now we could only dream about the good times we would have had. We both struggled to survive, grieving without each other to lean on.

Lee never talks a lot about her mom. She said it hurts too much. I'm glad she had Aunt Joyce. I wish I'd been there with her and Aunt Joyce instead of at that pet store. I could make them laugh. Where was Grand Master? Why didn't he help them?

Lee loved her mom. I can tell. Maybe more than I love Lee. Lee said she could tell her mom loved her. I guess I have her mom to thank for the way Lee loves and takes care of me! Maybe I'll see Lee's mom and Grand Master on my way to doggy heaven. I can thank her then! I miss Grand Master.

Among my many regrets was not doing enough to encourage a relationship between Cliff and my father, Leon. They first met at our wedding. Unfortunately, that was the last time. I kept thinking that they might have had a good time together. Cliff met my mom while we were dating. We traveled to Connecticut for a short visit with her and my aunt Viola. Since our relationship was getting serious, I wanted Cliff to know as much as possible about my family background. I had read someplace that when you marry someone, you marry the whole family. Cliff needed to know what he was getting into if we were thinking of a future together.

Although he had a great relationship with my godmother, who visited us regularly once we were married, Cliff didn't have a meaningful relationship with either of my biological parents. This added to my feeling of the brokenness of my bloodline, a feeling of disconnect. Now, it was too late. My dad died of respiratory complications in 1994, the same year Cliff was diagnosed with cancer. Regrettably, Cliff was unable to attend Dad's funeral due to his chemo treatments.

I didn't have a relationship with my dad until my adult years. He and Ma separated several months after I was born, but Ma talked about him often. She told me my father loved me and wanted me to live with him, but she wasn't about to let that happen. In fact, at one point, Ma refused to let my dad see me for fear he would try to kidnap me. Consequently, I didn't get a chance to know him until I graduated high school.

The summer of my graduation, a family friend, who had a connection with my father, arranged for me to travel by bus to my father's hometown in North Carolina for a visit. All that time, he was only a two-and-a-half-hour bus ride away. Looking back, this scenario seemed unimaginable. I had never stopped dreaming I would someday meet my dad. That dream was about to come true, and I was eager to take the trip. (Can you imagine traveling alone to a strange town to meet someone—sight unseen—who claimed to be your father?) Ma and my godmother trusted this family friend and encouraged me to go. Honestly, I think I would have gone even if they had been against it. I had no memories of my dad as a child—I was too young, and I was eager to get to know him. I was not about to lose this opportunity.

The bus ride was uneventful, but I will never forget what happened when I departed the bus. As soon as I stepped off the last step onto the platform where the bus parked, my eyes met this tall, dark, and rather handsome man whose face looked a lot like mine. We recognized each other immediately! After giving each other a brief, awkward hug, we headed toward his car, mostly in silence.

"Sarah is waiting for us with dinner on the table," he said, breaking the silence.

"Okay," I responded.

Dad had remarried not too long after divorcing my mom. Ma never wanted a divorce and was heartbroken for many years after they separated. So many years had gone by with no contact between them. My dad apparently placed an ad in the newspaper implying that he didn't know my mom's whereabouts and was seeking a divorce due to abandonment. This was common practice in those days, so I was told. If the spouse in question did not answer the ad after a lengthy deadline, the marriage could be dissolved. I can only imagine the pain my mother suffered when she found out that Dad had divorced her without her consent or, worst of all, her knowledge. She insisted whenever we talked about their separation that she never divorced my dad. I think she still had feelings for him after all those years. What a betrayal!

I liked Sarah, Dad's wife, though she looked nothing like I expected. First of all, she was much shorter, maybe about four feet nine or ten inches. Her skin was very fair, and her hair was cut in a long bob and dyed a bright reddish color. She could surely have passed for White.

Sarah was very kind to me and seemed to know all about me. She was the one who told me how she and my dad met as well as how he got a divorce. They met at a movie theater where she worked as a ticket clerk. Sarah was very open to discussing my mom—almost to the point of curiosity. My dad, on the other hand, was tentative and cautious in our conversations about the past. He was not quick to answer all my questions, but he wanted me to know, without a doubt, that he wanted me and that my mom wouldn't give him custody. I sensed the shame he had endured, so I tried not to add to his pain by pressing too hard to understand it all. I could wait. I knew right away that this would not be my last visit.

Dad owned a barber shop located in the heart of his community that could be seen from the front porch of his house. (His wife found it very convenient. When she needed something, she could literally call out to him if he were standing in front of his shop.) He was a fun-loving guy, and everyone I met had good things to say about him. I even got a chance to hang out with him at the shop for a few days, where I learned there is nothing like barbershop talk. My father was often the center of it all—opinionated and highly respected. He loved music and could often be heard whistling while waiting for the next person to take the chair. (I love music too. I was beginning to feel like my father's daughter.)

Over time, my dad and I developed a good relationship. It was obvious he felt guilty about not being there for me and tried very hard to make up for lost time. But how could he? He had missed seventeen years of my childhood. Nonetheless, I was happy to have him in my life and spent as much time with him as I could before heading off to college.

We continued to see each other throughout my college years, and he even traveled to upstate New York to escort me down the aisle on my wedding day, when Cliff and I married. Amazingly, on that day, we had the worst snowstorm seen in many years, even for December. My father declared he would never visit "that cold place" again. He never did.

I discovered while getting to know him that he, too, had a problem with drinking and had been sober for twenty years prior to our meeting. He started drinking excessively while in the navy. His and Ma's drinking habits were partly responsible for the destruction of their marriage. A few years before he died, he started drinking again, a decision that ultimately contributed to his poor health and demise. I considered it a blessing to have gotten to know my dad while he was sober. God always knows best.

My mom, my dad, my godmother, who died a few months before Cliff, and now Cliff—I wondered how much more I could withstand. It seemed like the curse of death was foremost in my life. Although it was very difficult dealing with the loss of my godmother, I found comfort in knowing she was not suffering any longer. She had been sick for such a long time. Being the woman of faith that she was, my godmother made it known that she was ready whenever God was ready to call her home. She died peacefully in the arms of her son, who had moved in to take care of her in her last days.

Cliff, on the other hand, was not ready and made it clear he wanted aggressive treatment until the end. He insisted I not let the doctors give up until all treatment options were exhausted. I truly believe he was afraid to die. The thought that he may have died in agony haunts me to this day. My prayer is that in the split second before his breath left him, God had mercy on him and filled him with peace.

My dad opted to continue drinking in spite of the damage to his lungs. And my poor mom never had a chance. Darkness had surrounded her for so long; she couldn't find the light. I pray that she did not feel alone when her spirit left this earth.

A TIME TO HEAL

Lee's getting better, but life's not the way it was before. I miss the old Lee. This Lee is not as much fun. I know Lee misses Grand Master—so do I—but it's time to play games again. Lee never feels like going out, even when her friends come by to see us. Sometimes, the phone rings, and Lee won't even pick it up. Sometimes she picks it up and puts it back down again. Lee says she is grieving—something you do when someone you love is gone and makes you sad.

I'm ready to play again! I love Grand Master like Lee, but a dog's gotta do what a dog's gotta do! Grand Master wouldn't want us lying around like two lost puppies. Grand Master was an alpha, strong like me. If he could talk to us, he would tell Lee to run free and take Coco for long walks and give Coco all the ice cream he wants to eat.

Thank goodness for Aunt Jean! Aunt Jean is what Lee calls a hoot! I don't know what that means…maybe it means she loves to play and have fun! She comes over when the sun is shining and when the sun is dark to take care of us. She always brings a lot of food. Yummy yum! Lee feels better when Aunt Jean is around. I like having her around too. She plays games with me, like running around the house. I run, and Aunt Jean tries to catch me. When we get tired *of playing and running around the house, Aunt Jean takes me for long walks—fast like Grand Master. I keep up!*

Lee says Aunt Jean is coming over to take me for a ride in her car. I like riding in her car. It's smaller than Lee's, and I can jump in and out by myself, like a hotshot! I keep my eyes to the window until I see Aunt Jean's car coming our way. Lee and I rush outside. No leash? When the car stops, and Aunt Jean opens the car door and gets out, I jump in ready to go! She goes over to talk to Lee and leaves the car door open. I can't believe it! What is she thinking? Is this a new game…to see if I will stay? I'm not waiting around for an answer. Before Aunt Jean can get back to the car, I jump out of the car and run down the walking trail like lighting! I wonder if Aunt Jean can catch me now! I can't believe what's happening! I have no leash! I am as free as a bird! Life is good!

When Aunt Jean sees me running so fast, she calls my name like Lee calls my name when I'm bad. "Cooooooooooocoooooooo!" Almost makes me come back. But no way! I don't want to stop playing this game! I look back, but I keep running. I see Lee running too. I guess Aunt Jean scared her like she did me. I stop to see what is happening. This is all new to me. Should I go back to the house or keep running? I want to go back. I don't want Lee to be mad. But I love running free with no leash. So I keep running.

I am never able to run free with no leash unless I am inside. Heck, the dog next door never has a leash—even outside! (Now I know why he is always so happy running in circles!) I love this new game! Lee and Aunt Jean try to catch me, but I am too fast for them. (If Grand Master could see me now, running so fast!)

I do love this game, but my legs are hurting. I don't see Lee and Aunt Jean, so I stop and lie in the grass. But the game isn't over. I see them coming again. Aunt Jean catches up with me first, and Lee circles around the other side to stop me before I run again. But I am too fast! I jump up and run down the street as fast as my short legs can take me. I guess Lee and Aunt Jean are getting tired now. They run back toward the house and jump into Aunt Jean's car. Looks like they are coming to get me!

The car stops right next to me. Lee gets out of the car and leaves the car door open. She has a cookie in her hand. You know how I love cookies! I'm getting tired of playing this game, so I grab that cookie, jump into the car, and stretch out on the seat. My body is moving up and down so fast! I have to wait until my body stops moving to eat my cookie. Lee gets in and puts me on her lap. Aunt Jen is sitting next to me. I thought we were having fun until I see Lee's eyes. They are big and round. I had seen this look before when she was scared. Water is coming out of Aunt Jean's eyes. Lee's eyes are wet, but there is no water on her face. I am confused. Lee looks mad. Who is she mad at? Is she mad at me? Still confused, I lick the cookie crumbs off my paws and close my eyes.

"Don't you ever do that again!" Lee says. She is loud. "Don't run away like that again."

I open my eyes and look at her. She looks sad. So this wasn't a game. Lee was scared of losing me, like she lost Grand Master. Putting one paw over one eye, I begin licking the other paw until it starts to ache.

The sun was unusually bright this particular morning. I could see, through sleepy eyes, its rays slowly forcing their way through the opening of drapes that hung loosely across the bedroom windows. Coco and I loved sunny days. Ironically, we both suffered from sun sensitivity. That didn't stop us from basking in it every chance we got. Coco was always eager to go outside, whether he had to potty or not. He loved exploring new territory and running as far as his leash would allow. I recall the time he ran away from me and Jean. I think he thought we were playing a game. I was so frightened. I knew that our backyard bordered a major highway, and there was no fence to stop him from running out into the road. My heart was pounding so fast that day! I don't know what I would have done if I had lost Coco.

The days didn't seem as long anymore. My heart still ached thinking about Cliff. I missed the Sunday-evening drives we used to take—always stopping somewhere to get ice cream. It was hard to think about the holidays I would have to spend alone. With God's help, I made it through Valentine's Day, but Easter was approaching soon. I was dreading it already. Cliff and Jean's husband, Cleave, liked planning special places for the four of us to eat on Easter Sunday, after church. We always had a great time. I knew Jean would try to get me out with them without Cliff. I hoped she'd understand when I refused. Being with couples is extremely difficult when you've lost your mate. It brings back so many memories and deepens your feelings of loss and loneliness. I shunned a number of invitations because of the pain. I just needed to hang in there. I knew things would get better with time.

I noticed that I was getting a little more sleep than usual. That was a good sign. One morning, it was approaching six o'clock, and Coco had been nudging me to wake up for quite some time. (By that time, he was a welcome guest in my bed.) He pranced from one end of the bed to the other, waiting for any hint that I was awake. When his wet nose brushed my face one time too many, I began to stir.

"Okay, Coco," I responded, yawning my way past his wagging tail. "I'm coming. Give me another minute please!" Coco would not take no for an answer. He kept wagging his tail all over my face, ignoring my plea. Reluctantly, I pulled myself out of bed, threw on my favorite jogging outfit, and headed toward the door. Coco was waiting impatiently with his leash hanging from his mouth, signaling he was ready to leave—without me, if necessary.

Walking Coco was getting easier. I was able to enjoy our time outside now, rather than feeling guilty because I really wanted to be back in my bed with the covers pulled over my head. I was so grateful I had Coco. God knew I was going to need him more than Cliff needed him. He didn't just send me a dog. He sent me a dog who was loyal and had a loving temperament. Coco was extraordinary. Everyone who met him wanted to be a part of his life or make him a part of theirs (except for my one friend who has a dog phobia, and my sister Joyce's husband, who basically ignored Coco when he was around…oh, and a former pastor, Pastor Ford, who never liked dogs of any kind, under any circumstances).

Coco had a way of wooing those who seemed a little cautious of him. He could always tell—dog instinct, I guess. Consider my cousin Marie: When Marie met Coco for the first time, she greeted him with the widest grin and strolled right past him without even a pat on the head. She sat as far away from him as possible. Well, Coco could tell she was a bit standoffish. He sashayed over to her and flopped at her feet like they were old buddies. It was not long before Marie reached down, gave him a pat or two on his head, and began speaking to him in that coochy coo voice (a no-no in our house) that emerges so spontaneously when talking to dogs and babies. Mission accomplished, Coco wandered off, tail wagging, to find the next victim.

Lee's not sad like before. I can tell. When the sun comes up, we go for long walks. Sometimes she takes me with her to the stores. I fall back in my seat a lot, but my legs keep pulling me up, and I sit up like before and see the trees. I sit on my hind legs, pull myself up, and put my nose on the right spot on the window to keep from falling. I can see the trees almost like before, when Grand Master was here to help me.

I love seeing the cars go by! Some move fast like me, and some move slow like Lee! Sometimes, a dog in another car looks my way. I don't want to bark, but these little pups can get me going. When they pull up to my window, I pull my head to the side and bark so much, Lee pulls my leash to get me back in my seat. But I get up on my hind legs like before when she looks away. Alpha dog!

I don't like it when we pass a dog helping his master drive. That dog sits up in his master's lap with his nose sticking out of the window for everyone to see. I look at Lee to see if she sees what I see. I want her to see that I can play the driving game too if she lets me. She never does.

When Lee is feeling lonely, she lets me ride in the seat next to her. Boy, I'm a happy dog! I pull myself up on my hind legs and look out the window with my head up high for all the dogs to see. One time, a man driving in front of Lee stopped driving. Lee did the same thing. She said she didn't want to hit his car. I fell out of my seat and hit the floor so hard, my ears started making these loud noises. My head felt like a spinning top. My poor legs wobbled as I tried to jump back on the seat. Lee thought I was hurt! She stopped driving, moved over to me, and rubbed every part of my body. Seeing the look in her eyes, I wagged my sore tail, telling her I was okay. That was my last ride in the front seat. The back seat had my name on it!

We are even beginning to settle into our bedtime routine again: stretch out on the big chair after we eat, watch the people in this big box, and nap until Lee is ready to go to bed. One time, Lee opened her eyes, jumped up like the house was on fire, and yelled, "Coco, wake up! We've got to go to bed!" She had a bad dream. She picked me up and carried me to my bed in another room. That didn't stop me! When it got quiet, I scooted into her bedroom, jumped on her bed, and crawled near her pillow. Lee didn't even yell at me. We fell asleep.

I couldn't put it off any longer. It was time for me to start thinking about going back to work. The school district had been so supportive and insisted that I take as much time as needed to get back on my feet. It had been almost three months since Cliff had passed. I missed him terribly, and I didn't feel ready to go back to work. But I knew I couldn't stay home forever. Maybe going back to work would help me think about something else other than death and sadness and being alone.

Fortunately, I wasn't suffering financially. Cliff had taken care to see that I had what I needed. What I wanted was to feel a sense of purpose and emotional security. My job as a school counselor was so demanding. The thought of dealing with other people's problems made me anxious. I wasn't handling my own too well. But I knew I would have to give it a try. I needed to move beyond my solitude and get back to socializing with others. I hoped going back to work would challenge me to push myself toward healing. I knew from previous losses that healing takes time. Yet I felt like I was running out of time, and I didn't want to lose my job, even though I was ambivalent about returning. As generous as my employer was, I couldn't expect it to keep my job open forever. My students needed stability; so did I.

Part of my game plan for getting back on my feet and getting back to work was to meet regularly with my counselor. I regretted having put it off for so long; however, it was not too late—it was never too late to ask for help. I promised myself I would take care of notifying the school district of my return date and set up an appointment with my counselor by the end of the day. Accomplishing that mission gave me a sense of satisfaction that moved me forward.

Getting back to work was harder than I expected it would be. I was so far behind. My students were eager to see me—my days were filled with appointments. I worked long hours, sometimes getting home after dark. No matter what time I arrived, Coco was eagerly waiting to go potty—some days were too close for comfort.

Before the school year ended, I was sure that I could not continue working in such a high-stress job. I was still fragile. I no longer had the energy to handle the daily problems of work and cope with the feeling of sadness that lingered. I continued to have trouble sleeping and was tired all the time. Sometimes, it was hard for me to remember when to take Coco out for his walks or to give him his treats. I was sure I was suffering from depression. I continued meeting with my counselor, but it was a long journey back to recovery.

I want Lee to be happy, take me for walks, feed me, and cuddle with me until I fall asleep. No matter how tired, she always takes good care of me. One time, I was sick. My stomach was doing flips, and I did my business on the floor before Lee could get to me. I could tell she wasn't happy, but she didn't yell at me or make me feel bad. She cleaned me up and talked in my ear, "I understand. We all get sick sometimes. Accidents happen."

Lee says she's going to see someone to help her get rid of this thing she calls depression—it makes her sad and tired. Boy, am I happy! I don't know who this person is, but I've done everything in my doggy power to make her feel better. It isn't working. I am worried—so worried I have a bald spot on my paw from licking so hard.

Lee says she needs to talk to someone who knows her friend Jesus. I wish I knew more about this man Jesus. Does He help dogs too? Maybe He will come by to see me when I go to that place where dogs go when they are good?

After a few sessions with my counselor, I was beginning to feel better. Things were starting to make sense to me. My heart reeked of so much sadness and anger, I was unable to make good decisions about my future. Talking to a Christian counselor helped me understand the cause of my depression and gave me hope. I was, at last, able to begin thinking about life as a widow. The thought of being alone—single again—filled me with anxiety and fear. Nonetheless, sharing my insecurities and disappointments with someone who could help me make sense of those feelings in a spiritual context was invaluable.

Counseling sessions helped me to understand that my profound grief was not just because of Cliff's passing. It was a culmination of the unresolved deaths I had endured previously and how I had processed death experiences throughout my life. My work with the counselor involved exploring the root cause of my fear, beginning with early childhood experiences.

Reflecting back, storytelling about haints, a southern word for ghosts, was a frequent theme in our house. Ma, Grandma, Papa, and some of my aunts often told us ghost stories at night before we were sent off to bed. We loved it—until one evening at dusk, when we were playing outside, Grandma yelled for us to come inside. It was getting dark. We ignored her and continued playing our games: Red Light, Green Light; Hide and Seek; and Rise Sally Rise. Out of nowhere came a white figure walking slowly toward us, waving its white arms in the air. Someone yelled, "Look! A haint!" We all ran toward the house like a flash of lightning, shoving each other as we reached the narrow door to be the first one inside. When we were all in, huffing and puffing to catch our breaths, my aunt Eve entered the house from the back door with an arm full of clothes she had retrieved from the clothesline outside. One item appeared to be a white sheet. Without saying a word, we looked at each other in silence, reading each other's minds: *Aunt Eve was the ghost*, we thought. But we couldn't be sure…

Somewhere between early childhood and life at the big house, I had another encounter with death that left a stinging impression. My maternal grandmother's sister, Aunt Dump, died. (We called her Aunt Dump because she was so short and dumpy.) Her death was my first experience with someone dying. Aunt Dump was my grandmother's only living relative known to us at the time. She lived in the country, a rural area miles away from our house. We never saw her much before her death.

It was common during the early fifties for the dead to be dressed and laid out at home. A huge plastic floral arrangement adorned the front porch of the deceased's house in their honor and notified all the neighbors of a death in the neighborhood. People living on the same street or road visited the family all hours of the day and night, bringing food and words of comfort.

Aunt Dump lived in a tiny row house (all the rooms were arranged in a row from front to back, also known as shotgun houses). During the "settin' up," a time when friends would visit the home and sit with the family, I recall sitting on the front row of chairs that faced the coffin—a coffin so large it appeared (through the eyes of a wide-eyed, frightened child) to consume the space of the entire room. I was only four or five at the time; I was horrified. We sat there in silence—it was called paying your respects—for what seemed like an eternity. The image of Aunt Dump dressed in her finest and housed in this monstrosity of a casket haunted me for years. For a long time afterward, I was afraid of the dead and anything that had to do with death.

To make matters worse, in our neighborhood, funeral homes were notorious for opening the doors of their parlors, which oftentimes faced the streets, to cool the hot air in the rooms—making it possible for those passing by to see the dead dressed in their coffins. So whenever there was a funeral home in my walking path, I would quickly cross over to the other side of the street to avoid such an encounter. As I got older, those fears subsided, but my discomfort with death persisted much longer.

Sadly, I experienced many deaths after Aunt Dump's demise. And in some cases, I was responsible for making funeral arrangements, a task that raised my blood pressure to new levels. When my dad died, my stepmother insisted that I take charge of making all the arrangements. She didn't feel that she had the strength to handle it. Although I completed the arrangements with little difficulty, once my father was laid to rest, I grew more and more despondent.

Although it was nearly five years later when my godmother transitioned, it seemed too soon. I was still mourning the loss of my mom and dad and didn't think I would survive another loss of a loved one. Losing my godmother was like losing part of my soul. I was relieved that she no longer suffered in pain; yet it was hard to conceive of going on with my life without her love and support. She was the reason, besides my faith in God, I was able to face the challenges in my life. I didn't have Coco at the time, and Cliff was approaching his late stage of cancer. Not having my godmother to lean on was unthinkable. Her encouraging letters, especially during Cliff's illness, and powerful prayers helped me to continue putting one foot in front of the other—to keep moving. The thought of not being able to call her when I needed to hear a comforting voice was hard to bear.

My godmother died in February 1999, and Cliff passed in November of that same year. Nearly eight weeks after Cliff's death, my younger sister, Faye, died of liver failure. She was only forty-six. Her terminal illness was a shock. Having just buried my husband, I was still determined to be strong for her daughter, my niece, Dawn. I knew how important it was to be there for her and to let her know she could lean on me.

Talking out my feelings with my counselor and reflecting on all these death experiences helped me to see that my grief was extensive, understandably so, and I needed to give myself time to heal before making life-changing decisions. I was not emotionally healthy enough to work as a school counselor again, at least not in the near future, but I needed to be productive. I needed a purpose to energize me to go on with my life.

I loved working with my students, but I was so fragile—I didn't trust myself to provide solid support to them. Some of my students were already struggling with serious issues, either at home or at school. I wouldn't be able to forgive myself if my issues compromised my ability to be a good listener, mentor, or support person at a critical time in their lives. As it was, some of their problems stemmed primarily from relationships with unhealthy adults. I didn't want to be one of them.

After a few months of sessions, it was clear that the best way to transition to a more normal life was to do something I loved—go back to school. After graduating undergraduate college, one of my academic goals was to earn a doctorate in education. At the time, I eventually wanted to become a college professor. I knew getting a PhD was the best educational track for that profession. However, that dream quickly vanished when I began working as a school counselor and, subsequently, got married.

Now that I had the time and money (due to my inheritance), thoughts of going back to school, being a student again, and furthering my education were exhilarating. It didn't matter that I would probably be the oldest student in the class. I was taught that you're never too old to learn. In my remaining counseling sessions, I began focusing on when to retire from my job as a school counselor and when to begin the application process for

graduate school. I had finally turned the corner away from grieving and toward healing. The journey was not over, but I saw a
light peering through the darkness.

*Lee's with her counselor. She's been gone for a long time. I guess I'll take
another nap. My eyes pop open when I hear someone at the door. Lee
rushes into the house, picks me up, and places me on her lap. I haven't
seen her this excited in a long time—so excited, she is forgetting about
my potty walk. I sit as still as I can while she talks and talks—and
talks. I am trying to hear what she is saying. I hear something about
college, writing papers, and a new start. None of it makes sense to me,
so I'll just keep my eyes on her eyes, hoping she'll see…it's potty time.
Sometimes, I have to thump my right paw against the floor over and
over again to get her to stop talking and take me out. She finally gets
it! She grabs my leash, and away we go!*

*Finishing my business, I lead Lee back to the house. Thinking
about all the talk about Lee going to a place she called college…I
wonder if she's lost it. (But that's what her counselor is for—to keep
her from losing it!) Maybe Lee's getting tired of spending too much
time with me and needs to get out of the house. If she asks me, I'll tell
her to go back to work. I know her work schedule, but this college
thing is new. I hear her friends say going to college is hard work and
a lot of time away from home. I'm getting worried. What's going to
happen to me? Who will feed me and take me out to potty when Lee's
gone for a long time? Lee says everything will be okay, but I'm not so
sure. When humans lose it, dogs don't stand a chance!*

As it turned out, going back to college was a great idea. I started taking classes slowly to ease into it. It had been almost twenty years since I finished my postgraduate classes to keep my certification for school counseling. Most of those classes were taken while working full time. Now, with early retirement at fifty-two, I would have the luxury of focusing on my studies full time. I knew I had made the right decision.

The great thing about going back to college was that it forced me to go out among people. I hadn't felt like socializing in a long time. Being around couples was still the toughest challenge. Having Coco was a blessing, but even Coco couldn't take the place of human companionship—though I tried hard to pretend I was okay. Going to classes, meeting new people, and having meaningful adult conversations were game changers for getting off to a new start. I embraced it fully.

Nighttime used to be our time. (I don't know about this college thing!) Lee is always too tired to play with me, so after dinner, we mostly watch the pictures on the big box on the wall. I like the pictures of the dogs playing and running free. They run so fast! It looks like they can run right out of that big box. (Reminds me of when I ran free from Aunt Jean and Lee.) I want to play with Lee like those dogs in the big box, but I don't want to wake her up from her nap. Like a good doggy, when Lee needs a snooze, I take a snooze. I stretch my body to let my head hang down from the side of the chair, snuggle next to her, and close my eyes. Soon, I am running free as a bird through a field. (I always have dreams about running free.

Only time I can run free without the old leash around.) I wonder what Lee dreams about when she closes her eyes.

Good thing is, Lee is having fun with other humans. Some of them come to see us. Lee lets me play with them! Chasing Coco around the house is my favorite game! They love it when I run, stay in one spot for a while, and take off running again around that table with the corners. Sure hope that table sees me coming!

DANCING WITH PEACE

Lee doesn't talk about her sadness much, but I know. Guess we dogs have a special sense about our mommies. We know when they need to be cuddled or licked on the side of their faces. (Lee and I don't play the lip-licking thing!) She loves college, but she still misses Grand Master. Bedtime is hard. She doesn't sleep much. Lee likes it when we stretch out on the big chair to take a nap until time to go to bed. She hates going to bed alone.

Sometimes when we're sitting on the floor waiting to get sleepy, Lee wraps herself in our favorite blanket. I keep my eyes on her. When she pulls me over, I put my head in her lap, and she gets close to my ear, "Coco, my sweetie pie." That's when I know she needs to talk. My ears are open wide, ready to hear Lee talk to me.

She talks a lot about God. "God has answered my prayers," she said. "I haven't lost a loved one in a while." I'm confused. I didn't know anyone was missing!

Some things Lee says don't make sense, like when she talks about dancing with death and dancing with peace. I look at her with my eyes wide open, like I know everything she's saying. What's a dog to do? I just want Lee to be happy, take me for my walks, and give me my cookies!

Most of the time, I was enjoying my new life. Somehow, I thought it would magically take away the grief. When that didn't happen, I began to lose faith and question my existence. All of those shortcomings, fears, and insecurities came flooding back. My hopes and dreams were shattered, or at least seemed so far away. I was confused by my lack of faith. God had showered me with so many blessings: Coco, a home, money to go back to school. I wanted to be able to handle my trials with strength and wisdom, trusting God. Yet I felt faithless—not as strong as I appeared to others. I wanted to be able to *let go and let God.*

I was spending more time in church, hoping to meet God face to face, I guess. The days that I didn't have classes were filled with mostly church activities. I even accepted a position as a church leader, a steward. Although I knew this was a demanding task, I felt I owed it to God to utilize my time, talent, and resources to His glory. He had blessed me in so many ways.

My counselor and I decided I could take a break from meeting for a while. She assured me she would be available if I needed a refresher. And I must say, I had become so busy lately, I needed to have some extra hours in my day to keep up. Church duties as a steward were consuming a great deal of my time. In addition, our church was designated to host the annual conference, and my pastor, Pastor Ford, had appointed me to serve on its strategic planning committee. The committee met often, and we all left the meeting with a list of tasks.

Church had become a place of security—the only place I felt a sense of peace. When Cliff died, members of the church embraced me and encouraged me not to be ashamed to express my grief and work through my pain. For a while, there were very few Sundays during church services that I didn't shed a river of tears. There was always someone there to comfort me and give me a hug. But I cried so much, it was getting to be embarrassing. Many times, I tried to hold back the tears to force a smile.

Members of the church had become my family, and I needed their support. As they prayed with and for me, my faith was strengthened, and my relationship with God gave me hope. It was not long before I began to experience a breakthrough in the healing process.

Lee is not the same. We have our talks. And Lee holds me in her lap, rubs my back, and talks in my ears about her troubles, but not like before. I guess she can see that spot behind my ear's getting bigger. Lee stopped talking about being alone and talks about her friend Jesus. She says what happened to Grand Master made her think about the love of Jesus. The love of Jesus makes the hurt in her heart go away. (I don't like hearing Lee talk about a man loving her and taking care of her. That's my job!) I guess I should be happy this man Jesus is here when Lee needs him.

Working on the conference committee turned out to be a life saver in more ways than one. Pastor Ford, who chaired the committee, made it a lot of fun. Since it was a small group, we got to know each other quite well. It was hard work, but we enjoyed the fellowship. The one single man on the committee, Henry (who was also a steward of the church), and I developed a nice friendship working together to complete certain duties. He had a great sense of humor and found lots of opportunities to tease me.

I recall the time I presented my selection of conference bags to be reviewed by the committee for their approval. Pastor Ford had warned us prior that we did not have a big budget to work with. Keeping that in mind, I searched for conference bags that were practical and not too costly. When Henry and Pastor Ford saw the samples that I presented, they both got a kick out of teasing me. Henry said the bags were low budget for sure. And Pastor Ford chimed in saying, "These bags are so practical, you can fold them up and put them in your pocket." I didn't quite see the humor, but I knew it had been a long day for everyone, and we needed to relieve some tension. I forced a smile and let them have their fun.

Before long, I knew there was a connection. Though Henry never made any moves to indicate a romantic interest in me, we were able to laugh and talk easily together. For the first time in a long time, I felt excited about the prospect of dating again—maybe not this man, but some nice man in the future.

At first, I found it difficult to contemplate being with anyone else. Although my early marriage to Cliff was challenging, after our separation, we recommitted ourselves to do whatever needed to be done to care for each other. By that time, we had been married for nearly twenty years. After living with someone for so many years, it was hard to even think about having another man in my life. It had been almost four years since Cliff's death. Until now, I was content exploring life on my own terms (not to mention that I was too fragile emotionally to have a healthy relationship with anyone). I had forgotten how nice it felt to socialize with another male. My friendship with Henry gave me hope.

Lee's gone a lot. When she's at home with me, we play games like chase the ball and find the shoe. I can tell she's happy now. Her eyes are not wet like before. She takes me for long walks and lets me eat table food that falls on the floor. She turns her head to keep from watching me.

Lee talks a lot about a game called dating. She told me dating was when two people spend a lot of time together to see if they like each other. (Can dogs play this game?) I heard Lee say a lot of people play the dating game on something called the internet. What's an internet? Do dogs play dating on the internet? Where is it? Maybe that cute little puppy at Puppy Paradise will be there! I can have some fun like Lee!

OH HAPPY DAY

The annual conference committee meeting adjourned early, so some of us gathered in the church parking lot to socialize. I could see Henry talking to another man near his car. Ella (a friend who was not a member of the committee but happened to be at church for choir rehearsal) and I were conversing about my trip to France several months ago. One of my dear friends, Reverend Terry, had persuaded me to take a riverboat cruise with her to the south of France. She said I needed a vacation from all of my stress. While docked at designated ports, we took lots of pictures of the beautiful landscape, particularly the vibrant lavender gardens in Provence. I invited Ella to my home to see the pictures. I hadn't invited many people over since Cliff's death. But I thought it was about time I tried to reach out more to my family and friends. I felt ready.

Henry apparently overheard our conversation. "You've never invited me over," he interjected in a teasing manner.

Stunned, without any thought, I responded, "Oh, you can come too."

"What about Friday night?"

"Well, I guess that would be okay."

"What time?"

"I'll be home all day."

"It's a working day for me, so I'll call you later to confirm a time. Okay?"

"Okay."

I didn't know if he were still teasing, but I was amazed that I went along with the game. It felt nice to even think someone—a man—was flirting with me. I hadn't dated in so long, and I sure wasn't looking for someone at this time in my life. But replaying the conversation with Henry in my mind was intriguing and exciting.

Was he teasing or not? Before I went to France, we had communicated in a string of unusual emails about how I would miss the fish fry he was giving to celebrate his graduation but that he would freeze some for me until I returned. (Henry had earned his master's degree while studying part time at a local university.) Though I don't recall the details of the emails, I remember us both responding to each other in a vague but flirtatious manner. (Afterward, Henry confessed he was just being friendly.) So did he really want to come by, or was he just being *friendly*? Why did I say yes so quickly? Did I sound eager, like I was interested in him? What if he really was teasing? I felt like such a jerk! Oh well, what was done was done. I decided to stop torturing myself and wait to see if he called.

And he did!

I'm busy doing what I do when Lee is away. That spot in Lee's room that feels like the sun—that spot is for me! I love that spot. It makes

me feel warm all over. I can hear birds singing, but they know not to get in my way. One time they did. I ran to the window, barked like a mad dog, and those little guys couldn't get away fast enough! They flew like the wind!

I was snoozing in that sunny spot when the sound of Lee's car woke me up. I must have been napping for a long time. (Or maybe she missed one of her classes!) I hear the door open, but I'm having too much fun being lazy to go check it out. (I gotta keep Lee on her toes.) She comes in singing my name. "Cocomo! Wheeeeeere aaaaaaare youuuuuuuuuuuuuuu?" (What's wrong with this lady? When she calls me Cocomo, I know something's up. Did she forget about my snoozing in the sunny spot? It's a sunny day! This is what I do on a sunny day!)

Lee sounds so happy, and her face is smiling. She takes her jacket off and puts her books on the chair. I follow her around the house like a poor puppy dog, waiting for her to talk, talk, talk.

Oh boy! That face looks like...when Grand Master was with us. The same smile! Lee is in love! But wait! Jesus is the only man Lee talks about. But she said Jesus is in our hearts. We can't see him, but we can feel him! So who is this man? How could she hide him from me? What about my say in this? What would Grand Master say? Had she lost it...again?

When Lee sees me, she almost steps on my paw. I see her eyes move around in a way I haven't seen before, and her face is shining—not tired or sad looking. She is smiling from one side of her face to the other.

"You lazy dog," she says, sitting down on the floor next to me. "We've got to hurry. I've got a date! We'll have to make this a short walk today."

I can't believe my doggy ears! What's she saying? We have to make this a short walk? We'll see about that! (I have my ways of making our walks longer when I want more time.) I walk very slowly, like I am so tired, and just mess around. When I find a spot to do my business, I move around in circles until I just can't hold it anymore. Lee is not happy. She catches on and gives my leash a hard pull. "Let's go, Coco!" pulling my leash even harder.

I pull back on my leash and circle some more like I have to go potty again. I take my doggy-loving time, until I see that look in her eyes; I take care of business fast and walk ahead of her, never looking back. I know she's upset. Don't much care!

Walking back to the house, I begin thinking: What if this man does not like dogs? What if he wants to get rid of me and get one of those big dogs? Some men don't like us cute little guys. At the pet store, the men played games with the big dogs all the time. But not Grand Master! He wanted me!

When we get home, Lee hands me my cookie. "I want you to meet someone. He's coming over to see us tonight," she says.

Hold on! Wait a minute! You want me to meet someone tonight? Lee's losing it! This is not the way to treat your best friend in the whole world! I have no time to get myself ready! Maybe I need my hair brushed so he'll like me! When do I get to eat my grain bowl? What about our bedtime routine?

It must be that nice man from the church! Lee used to talk about him a lot. Maybe they've been playing the dating game without telling me. I don't like Lee surprising me, but I'm happy for her. Maybe she's tired of talking to a dog. I know my ears need a rest, but I'm afraid of someone taking my place. What will I do without Lee? I'm the man of the house—well, me and Jesus, who never even comes around unless Lee calls him! Maybe if I call Jesus, this nice man from the church will go home.

I must admit, I was shocked when Henry called to say he would be over at seven. Guess he wasn't teasing after all. I was so nervous! Choosing something to wear was a challenge. I wasn't sure if I should go a little dressy or casual. I hadn't invited him for dinner, but I wasn't sure if I should cook dinner anyhow or just prepare a few snacks. My mind was racing! Was this dating stuff worth the trouble? And Coco wasn't cooperating at all! I thought he'd be happy for me. Instead, he was moping around like he'd lost his best friend—but he still wasn't letting me out of his sight. I wondered if he thought I would leave him, like I did when Cliff died.

Coco had been through so much. Henry would have to like him, or he would have to go! But it would take some time. I needed to give him some time to get to know Coco. Then I was sure he would love him like I did. Everybody loved Coco…Wait a minute! I was going on about Henry liking Coco. What about me? What if he found out that he really didn't like me, except for as a friend? I was getting way too far ahead of myself. Taking a long breath, I decided to take things one step at a time: no food, no change of clothes—just be myself. Besides, it wasn't even a real date. Henry was just dropping by!

GUESS WHO'S COMING TO DINNER

You have to be in the house to get the picture: In walks a man who looks like one of those pictures I saw one time on the big picture box. They call them giants! I can hardly breathe! I watch him for a long time, my eyes moving wherever he moves. I have never seen such a big fellow in my doggy life! (I call him Big Fellow. Lee calls him Henry.) I raise my head up as high as it will go to see his face. And he has big hands and big feet! (Watch out, paws!) I can't understand why Lee wants to play the dating game with such a big human. Big Fellow is too big for Lee! I don't have to raise my head up to see Lee's face like with Big Fellow. (Reminds me of that big dog at Puppy Paradise who's always running behind this little pup.) My head moves back and forth between Lee and Big Fellow like I am playing a game.

My head moved around so much, Lee thought I was sick. I'm surprised she looks my way. No, I'm not sick. I'm just trying to keep up with what's going on. I want Lee to have a man in her life, but... What if he tries to be the man of the house? Does she need someone else to take care of her? I'm a little fella, but I know how to keep her safe. I have a good bark and a great bite. Maybe I'm just having a *hard time…Lee might stop needing me, with a man like Big Fellow around.*

Lee tells me he's her friend and tells him I'm Baby Coco. I guess she forgot I'm the man of the house, or maybe she's sending me a message that she's getting a new man of the house. I'm not happy about what's going on!

Big Fellow comes close to me. I back up real fast—so fast, I bump into the wall behind me. What's he doing? He doesn't know me to get that close! I'm surprised when Lee picks me up and lets him rub my head without asking me. I'm not ready for him to touch me, but I don't want Lee to know, so I let him rub away. When Lee puts me down, I run as fast as I can to the bedroom. I know he won't come into our bedroom—will he?

I wait without making a sound in my corner of the bedroom. I hear Lee laughing. (Big Fellow must be a funny man!) Lee sounds so happy. I want to be happy for her. But is he the right one for Lee? Lee's so special. She needs the right fellow to make her happy.

I can't wait any longer. I need a nap, but my eyes won't stay closed. I listen to what is going on. Silence. I walk to the room where I hear some noise. I see Lee and Big Fellow sitting on the big chair, and I jump right next to them. I guess they're surprised…looking at each other like they don't know who I am. They both smile.

I let Big Fellow rub my head again after he pulls me closer to him. Well, he seems to be a nice guy. I'm surprised at how soft his hands are. Maybe I'm wrong about him. Not moving, I sit next to both of them while Lee talks about her trip. She said that was the reason Big Fellow was coming over—that, and to play the dating game. I hear these stories about her trip a lot when Lee talks to her friends. I don't need to hear them again. But I'm not moving! I want Big Fellow to know I'm the man of this house!

Lee and Big Fellow are having a lot of fun. They laugh a lot! When Lee finishes talking about the trip, Big Fellow asks her to go for ice cream…without me! I'll bet they came up with that little plan when I dozed off. I'm so tired of hearing about those beautiful hillsides and the delicious French food, I don't care where they go. It's my bedtime.

The night had gone even better than expected. Henry was a perfect gentleman. And he really liked Coco! I told him not liking Coco could be a deal breaker. I guess he took it to heart. We spent hours getting to know each other while enjoying our ice cream at Friendly's, one of my favorite ice cream spots. Henry was an ice cream lover like me.

I was amazed at how easy it was for us to talk to each other. We shared many stories about our childhood, growing up in big families, our favorite movies, and our love of music. Henry shared that he had a son named Mark who was in junior high school at the time. Mark lived with Henry, but also spent time with his mom regularly, who lived in Illinois. In fact, I had seen Henry at church with his son long before Henry and I became acquainted.

Henry was a great jazz fan. I knew very little about jazz but could sing most of the words to any soul tune from the sixties and seventies. Listening to artists like the Temptations, Michael Jackson, The Four Tops, The Whispers, Gladys Knight, Patti LaBelle, Aretha Franklin, and my all-time favorite, Tina Turner, was the highlight of my college days. Henry was a native of Detroit, the music capital of that era, and had attended many concerts featuring most of these performers. I was delighted to hear how much we had in common. We both loved good food, great music, dancing, and traveling.

What sealed the deal for me was Henry's faith. Having met each other at church, I knew he was a church-going man. What I didn't know was the depth of his devotion. Ironically, we discovered we had attended the same church years ago, but due to the size of the church, our paths never crossed. I was married to Cliff at the time. In fact, the pastor of this same church officiated our wedding. Cliff and I left that church after a few years, in search of a smaller, more intimate congregation. Ironically, that same church is where I met Henry.

It was getting late, so Henry and I decided to head back to the house. We couldn't believe how fast time had passed. I was smitten with him and could not wait to see him again. I hoped he felt the same way.

I hear the front door shut. Big Fellow comes in. I hear the front door shut again. Big Fellow must be gone. I walk in and see Lee moving around the room like I do when I'm dizzy. Turning around and around, she falls on the bed on her back, stretches her arms from one end of the bed to the other, and looks at the ceiling until I start barking. I'm confused. Is she losing it again, or is she sick? She forgot it is past my potty time. I waited long enough. I'd better help her remember. I start chewing on the shoes falling from her feet until Lee gets up and grabs my leash. I follow her to the door. My time is getting too close. She takes me out for a quick potty, and I go back to my snoozing. I can still hear Lee moving around. She is making

those happy sounds again. I put my paws over my ears. The house gets quiet.

Taking care of Coco, keeping up with my coursework, dating: suddenly my life had become more demanding than I ever expected. Henry had a very challenging job, so we decided to see each other on weekends only. Yet we talked for hours nearly every night—sometimes during the day if there were time. We loved talking to each other about everything. I was able to get into heavy conversations about my deepest fears, my biggest regrets, and my greatest disappointments. He understood. There were even times he understood what I wanted to say before I could get my thoughts together—he was such a good listener.

I had not been able to share with anyone, except my counselor (and Coco), how lonely I was and how alone I felt when Cliff died. Henry listened intently. He wasn't judgmental, didn't try to dismiss my feelings, and was aware of how important it was for me to talk about Cliff. Therefore, he never interrupted me before I could get my words out—no matter how long it took. Having that kind of support and encouragement was just what I needed. His responses were gentle and caring.

As Henry and I got to know each other better, I decided not to talk about Cliff too much. I didn't want Henry to think that I was not ready for a new relationship. It had been almost four years since Cliff had passed. I was ready. Yes, it was a big adjustment, since I had not dated anyone else. But I needed to move on with my life. I realized during one of my counseling sessions that grieving was a long, slow process. Moving on with your life was important for healing to take place. I had already experienced too many moments of guilt and even anger, trying to make sense of how and why my life had become so full of tragedy. I knew God had a plan for my life beyond the suffering. I just needed to have faith and be patient.

It was a relief to see Henry and Coco getting along. I needed them to like each other. It made everything so much easier. My relationship with Henry had developed into a very strong friendship. He was a kindred spirit—my soulmate, a phrase I used frequently to describe him. Not sure I was in love, but I was certain that I was attracted to him. His gentleness, patience, and dependability were exactly what I needed during this season of uncertainty. God had answered my prayer—again. I was so grateful.

BIG FELLOW AND ME

Big Fellow is always around. We're getting to be best buddies. (Not like it was with Grand Master! No one can take his place!) He loves walking me like Grand Master, but Big Fellow doesn't walk me so fast. That's okay. I'm not as young as I used to be, so a slower walk is all I need.

Lee tells me she wants me to stay at Big Fellow's house while she goes on a trip with her friends. She drops me off, but Big Fellow leaves me alone to go to work. When he closes the door, I run up some steps to look around. No steps at our house, so I want to have some fun. I get to the top of the steps, and I can't get back down. I try, but the old paws keep slipping, and I'm afraid I will fall and break my neck! I don't want Big Fellow to come home and see me like this, but what's a dog to do when he's stuck? All I can do is wait.

When Big Fellow comes home and sees me stretched out at the top of the stairs, he doesn't look mad! I thought he'd be mad that I wasn't a good boy when he left me alone. When he calls me down and sees I can't come down by myself, he walks up to get me. He even has a smile on his face. That's my kinda guy! All I need now is to go potty.

I like staying at Big Fellow's house. (It's better than seeing those two nice ladies at Puppy Paradise.) He gives me all the food I can eat whenever I want it. Feels like home…well, almost! Lee only gives me one cookie at a time.

Life was beginning to take on a different meaning for me. Henry and I had been officially dating for more than a year now. We had our ups and downs as we were getting to know each other more intimately, but we were committed to each other, dating exclusively. We openly shared our concerns and made time to resolve any misunderstandings that arose. Since both of us were so busy, it was important to schedule time to be together. I remembered how not spending enough time with Cliff affected our marriage. I didn't want us to make the same mistake.

I looked forward to Henry's Friday-night visits. He was usually tired, and by the time he reached my house, at least forty minutes away, he was ready for a nap. It became a routine: after greeting each other with a hug and a kiss, Henry played with Coco for a while—or took him for a short walk, if needed—while I put the final touches on our dinner. After dinner, we settled in for a quiet evening, sharing the highlights of our week or listening to our favorite music. If we had the energy, we danced to tunes that had special meaning to us. I loved dancing; so did Henry.

Sometimes Coco and I traveled to Henry's house for dinner, usually on Sundays. Henry was a good cook, and he loved grilling. After dinner, we listened to music or watched a movie. Coco was always somewhere between us, until he couldn't take it any longer and slipped away to his favorite spot for a nap.

As we spent more time together, it was clear that Henry and I needed to talk about our future. Those conversations were tough. Henry was devoted to me but was not sure he was ready to get married. I, on the other hand, could not see myself in a long-term relationship without a commitment to marry at some point. There was too much at stake. It was clear that we didn't want to lose each other. We decided to give ourselves more time.

I guess Big Fellow is here to stay. It's been a long time, and they still have that look in their eyes! Lee is busy with that college thing and taking care of me; there's no time to take care of Big Fellow too. We'll see! I hear love makes humans do strange things!

Lee is spending more time with Big Fellow and less time with me. I see them cuddling a lot. I thought that was my job! Boy that makes me mad. I guess Lee needs Big Fellow more than me. He can do things for her I can't do—cook her good food, help her with college work, take her outside to play games (I only get to play games with her inside), and that thing Lee calls dancing. I wish I could move around the floor with Lee like Big Fellow. I like looking at Big Fellow circle around Lee like I circle around when I have to go potty. (I wonder if Big Fellow has to go potty.) I'm happy Big Fellow can do things for Lee that I can't do. Sometimes Big Fellow circles around too close to Lee. I guess I'm getting used to it. Like a good old dog, I have to go with the flow.

Big Fellow is around like he's part of the family. Now I run to the door to see him like I do when Lee comes home! We have a routine: Big Fellow walks in, I bark one time and run to our room where we play, and I wait for him to follow. He runs after me all around the room, over and over again. Sometimes, if he gets tired, he walks fast like he's running. He tries to catch me, but I'm too fast. I may be a little guy, but nobody can beat me running!

I can tell I'm slowing down some, but it won't stop me from playing cat and mouse. Sometimes I run past Big Fellow and stop for a while. When Big Fellow comes after me, I start running again. He misses every time. I know he lets me get away from him cause I'm not fast like I was with Grand Master. I wonder if Big Fellow knows I'm not as fast.

I can tell Big Fellow and Lee like this dating game. They hug a lot. I'm not ready for that, but I'm tired of leaving the room when Big Fellow comes around. Sometimes I stay. One time I stayed a little too long and Big Fellow hugged the breath out of Lee. Her face was getting red. (Time to go!) I ran to my corner in our bedroom. I didn't want to see Lee get mad and yell at Big Fellow.

The thing about relationships is, no matter how good they seem, there's always some hurdle to overcome. I was getting close to completing my coursework at the university and looking forward to a new chapter in my career. My goal was to establish a small counseling practice upon graduating. I didn't want to go back to work full time; however, I still had the energy and motivation to help others. And I had learned so much, academically and personally. Pursuing my own practice would give me the flexibility I needed to fulfill my desire to be of service to those in need of mental health support. Furthermore, I had planned to relocate—to start anew—in a different environment. I thought I had it all figured out. The problem was, Henry was still working.

He had a few more years before retirement and preferred I remain in upstate New York until he retired. We could relocate together. But he had three more years!

No matter how hard we tried to work it out, we couldn't reach a solution that pleased both of us. The tension was starting to wear on our relationship. Henry wanted me to follow my dream but wasn't sure how a long-distance relationship could survive. And I didn't want to delay my plans, especially without us committing to marriage. Once again, we decided to give it a little more time. I was so excited about planning my graduation weekend, and I didn't want the conflict we were having to spoil the great celebration we were expecting. Truth is, I didn't want *anything* to get in the way. I was happy to delay all discussions about our future until my celebration weekend was over.

A TIME TO CELEBRATE...OR NOT

May 2008—my graduation had finally arrived! I was ecstatic. I had forgotten all the hard work and the late nights of crying and praying to be done with this. It was over! My childhood dream had become reality—I was Dr. Lee! Earning my PhD was a lifetime achievement, and I was so proud of my accomplishment. There were so many people to thank who helped me along the way: my sponsor, Dr. D. (as I affectionately called her); Henry, who encouraged me and helped me so much with the technology demands; and of course my sweet little Coco. He never made me feel guilty when I got home too late to feed him or take him out to potty.

Henry and I had planned a weekend of activities that included family members and close friends. Guests traveled from as far away as Texas, California, Michigan, and Connecticut to help us celebrate. It was a joyous occasion. The fun started on Friday night with a fish fry at Henry's house—lots of fish! Saturday morning until noon, we hosted an open house at my house. Then we were off to the graduation ceremony. The finale was on Saturday night at the country club in Henry's neighborhood—a dinner and dance with lots of grazing stations. It was perfect!

Lee's getting something from college called a PhD. I still don't know what that is, but if Lee's happy, I'm happy! I could find out about this PhD if Lee would let me stay around for the fun. But no way! She takes me to my other home with the two nice sisters. Lee says she wouldn't be able to take care of me with all the people around. I bet Lee is sending me away so I won't be around one of her friends who's afraid of dogs. When I heard Kate was coming to the party, I knew she would send me away. One time when Kate came to see Lee, I heard Lee tell her that I was a good dog and not to be afraid. I was confused! How could anyone be afraid of a little dog like me? I would not hurt a fly—unless it sat on my tail and refused to leave when I wagged it. Then that fly would be toast!

While Lee is having fun with her friends at her party, I'm having fun running around with all my doggy buddies. We like running around the yard. We play catch the ball. We like playing games with the nice ladies too. When they come around to take us back to our cages for our routine naps, we circle around in our cages like we have to potty. The nice ladies keep going back and forth taking us to the yard until we are all back outside running around again. Humans!

The best time is playing in the water! The nice ladies like to take us to play in the water when the sun is warm. If I'm not tired or sleepy, I watch the other dogs splash around and get each other wet. At home, I never get to play in the water. I only get wet when Lee takes me to the pet store for a bath. She's afraid water will make it hard for her to take care of my hair. Funny—they take care of my hair just fine at the pet store. Poor Lee!

This time, I'm getting in the water! Lee's not here to stop me! She's having fun at home without me! The nice lady opens my cage door, and I shoot out of there and run like a squirrel. I jump over one of the pups and hit that water like I own the place. Boy! What fun! Getting tired, I jump out of the water and shake my body so much— water goes everywhere! I run over to play with the other dogs—grabbing their tails and bumping into them until they bark me away. What a good time! Maybe coming back again won't be so bad!

Several months after the graduation celebration weekend, the honeymoon was over. Henry and I hadn't spoken for weeks. After that grand weekend slipped away, the future of our relationship was on the line. Truthfully, I was getting restless. I had finished my degree and was getting excited about the prospect of establishing my own business. Several former students who were in their late twenties at that time had reached out to me in the past for counseling. They were struggling with career decisions, stressful marriages, and parenting issues and needed someone to talk to. So I knew there was a need. Starting my own counseling resource center seemed like a logical avenue for me to use my skills, knowledge, and frankly, what I learned from my personal experiences coping with some of those same concerns.

Henry and I agreed to pause our relationship to give us time to fully digest what was at stake. We were both unsure of how a long-distance relationship would work or survive. Neither one of us wanted to get hurt along the way. Not having a commitment to get married in the near future was not the lifestyle that reflected my Christian values, nor was it the life I believed God had planned for me. Henry knew and respected my position, but we couldn't reach a compromise.

By this time, we had been dating exclusively for almost four years. Eventually we agreed that we had no choice but to call it quits. As difficult as it was, we resolved to maintain a friendship and to be there for each other if there was ever a need. He was still my soulmate.

Big Fellow isn't around much anymore. The phone rings, but Lee won't talk. The happy look in her eyes is gone. She takes me walking a lot, even when I don't have to do my business. And Lee is at home a lot. Strange! After one of our long walks before our bedtime routine, Lee tells me that Big Fellow isn't coming to see us anymore. (I knew something was up.) I guess they are tired of playing the dating game—humans are like that, you know. I don't know why Lee took so long to tell me. Maybe it hurts too much. Poor Lee!

I'm getting worried again. Life isn't the same without Big Fellow. It feels like when Grand Master left. I don't get a lot of playtime with Big Fellow gone. Lee takes me out, but I can tell she's not happy. She forgets my treats and walks too slow. Same thing happened when Grand Master went to that place humans go when they are good. Who said a dog's life is easy?

With Big Fellow gone, I have to take care of Lee! I can't let Lee get sad again, like when…you know…when her eyes were wet, and she wore her nightgown all the time. (I hope I can make her happy like Big Fellow.) Lee was always happy when Big Fellow was around. That look in her eyes is gone without Big Fellow. Where is Aunt Joyce when I need her?

It was official! I was moving to the Carolinas again, but this time permanently! I had finally accepted my fate of breaking up with Henry. It was hard, but it had to be done. We were moving on without each other. Having grown up in North Carolina, I was looking forward to reconnecting with old friends who lived in the area. I had done a lot of research about some of the cities not far from my hometown, and I decided to look for an apartment in Charlotte, North Carolina. Charlotte was known as the New York City of North Carolina during my childhood. It was more progressive than the surrounding towns—especially in the education community—and offered a variety of events and activities for entertainment. Furthermore, the Charlotte area was surrounded by other locations within a three-to-four-hour drive for vacationing: Myrtle Beach, South Carolina; Atlanta, Georgia; Savannah, Georgia; Charleston, South Carolina—all places I was looking forward to spending time before making a final decision about a permanent location. I was determined to make this my last move.

It took a little longer than I expected to sell the house. The country was just starting to rebound from a crash in the banking industry and the housing market, and buyers were reluctant. I knew it wasn't the best time to sell at a big profit, but I was happy to break even. When a cash offer was presented, I took it!

Next step: find a new place to live!

Lee says we're moving to sunny North Carolina. I can't believe my ears! I know things aren't the same, but this is one big surprise! Lee is cleaning and moving things around and putting things in boxes a lot. She's moving my things around too. I can't find my bowl or my favorite toy slipper. Is Lee trying to forget Big Fellow by leaving town? Seems strange to me. How can you let someone run you out of town because they stop coming around? I miss Big Fellow too, but not enough to run away from home. Poor Lee! She has lost it this time!

It had been a long time since I lived in an apartment, and I had some reservations about how well Coco would adjust. However, I didn't want to invest in buying a house until I had a chance to explore the landscape in Charlotte and the cities nearby. Luckily, I was able to secure an apartment during a promotional season, which lowered my monthly rent substantially. The date had been set, and I was ready to go!

Joyce and Jean were traveling to New York to help me drive to North Carolina. (Jean and Cleave had already moved to Florida not too long after Cliff's death.) We had it all planned. We would leave New York on Sunday morning, spend the night somewhere about halfway down, and complete our drive the next day. Should have been a piece of cake with three people driving. What we hadn't anticipated was the big Saturday-night snowstorm. All the weather channels had warned us of an impending historic snowfall. But we were set on following our plan. We were ready to roll!

HITTING THE ROAD

Lee, Aunt Joyce, Aunt Jean, and Coco! How lucky can a fellow get? All my favorite people (except Grand Master and Big Fellow) in the car together! I can feel the cold air moving my tail. The fluffy white stuff touches my cheeks as I jump into the car—and we're on our way! Aunt Joyce and Aunt Jean sit in the front seat. Lee and I sit in the back. Lee sleeps a lot while I see the fluffy white stuff falling faster and faster. I want to get a lick, but Aunt Jean won't open the window.

Aunt Joyce drives so long, my legs hurt when I try to stretch them. All I know is I have to go potty now! Never mind the fluffy white stuff. I like walking in it when I go potty. The cool, wet feeling under my feet make it easy for me to do my business. Strange, huh? I love playing in the fluffy white stuff. I can run and play and…I feel a tug on my leash—it's time to go. I don't know why we have to hurry. I know I'm just a dog, but I don't think that place Lee calls North Carolina is going anywhere!

My eyes are getting tired of looking at the big cars buzzing past us. Guess it's time for another nap. A loud noise wakes me up. Eyes wide open, I jump to my feet. Everyone is getting out of the car, *closing the doors as they leave—leaving me behind! What the...I can't believe they're leaving me alone! In the car! In the cold! No heat! No food! And what about the cookies?*

I lose it! Lee can tell. She comes back to the car, scoops me into her arms, and heads for the door of a house. Where are we? Lee forgets—it is potty time. Back out the door we go. Lee carries me in her arms and puts me down on a grassy spot that is covered with slippery cold stuff. I slide when she puts me down.

"Go quickly," she whispers. "It's very cold out here."

I am eager to please!

We traveled about eight hours before reaching West Virginia, where we decided to stop to rest for the night. It was hard to find a hotel room due to the unexpected snowstorm, which had caused a power outage in the area. Nearly all rooms were booked by residents escaping a cold and dark house. After driving around for quite some time, we arrived at a hotel that had only one room left—a room left open for emergency use. The room looked as if it hadn't been cleaned, but we had no choice but to take it if we wanted to get some sleep before morning. It was already past midnight, so we swallowed our pride—for just one night.

I reluctantly put Coco's bed in a little corner of the room and wrapped him in his favorite blanket. It had been a long ride, and Coco had kept his eyes on us, refusing to sleep, except for short naps. All tucked in, he fell asleep in no time. I could even hear him snoring, which he only did when he was very tired. Sleeping in this room was much harder than we thought. We kept looking around to see if there were any creepy crawlers. Tossing and turning, we realized that none of us could sleep.

"Let's go," I finally said. "Since we can't sleep, we might as well keep driving." Joyce and Jean nodded their heads in agreement. We had never undressed, so we hurriedly put on our shoes and collected the few items we had with us. I picked up Coco while Jean grabbed his bed and blanket. As we reached the car, Joyce remembered that we needed to pay the bill. So she drove around to the front of the building to let me run inside to pay the bill. And off we went…before the sun came up!

I'm just a dog. But even a dog knows what just happened is crazy! It's bedtime! I'm snuggled in my blanket with my eyes closed and ready to run free. Before I can get out in the field, Lee is ready to go! Nobody asks me if I am ready to go! Humans! Lee puts me in the back seat, and I find a spot on the seat to lay my head, close my eyes, and…lights out!

The highway was crisp with the fallen snow, and there was a silence that pierced the entire atmosphere. The beauty of the sun coming up on a cold wintry morning was absolutely breathtaking! Not saying a word to each other, we drove along in a trance. What was not being said was said loudly and clearly: We were awestruck by such a beautiful sight! It wasn't long before we crossed the state line into North Carolina. Joyce was driving while Jean entertained Coco. He was getting restless, and we knew it was time to give him a potty break. Jean tried to settle him down until we could reach a nearby rest stop.

I need to go! Not sure how much longer I wait to do my business. Don't they see me walking from one end of the back seat to the other? I don't care if I am walking all over Aunt Jean's lap. When a dog's gotta go potty, nothing else matters. I thought Lee knew that by now!

Aunt Jean jumps out of the car, walks over to my side, and grabs me before Lee can get to me. It feels good having the ladies fighting over me. Lee leaves us, and Aunt Jean takes me for a walk. (Aunt Jean says Lee has to go potty too!) That fluffy white stuff is still on the ground, but my paws aren't sticking to the ground like our last potty stop. I'm not sliding…aaaaaaaaaah.

Aunt Joyce is still driving. What about Lee? Can't she drive sometime? Maybe she's afraid she will slide on the fluffy white stuff. I see a lot of cars on the road. Lee says people are trying to get to a place to work. Lee went to work before Grand Master left us. My eyes are wide awake, and my little head is bobbing all around, watching the cars go to work. Aunt Joyce stops at a light so the other cars can go. I come eyeball to eyeball with a little pup in a car next to us. And the barking begins! We bark at each other, making a lot of noise, until Aunt Joyce drives away. Too bad… I was ready to play the dog-eat-dog game!

I wake up from my snooze when I hear the ladies laughing and clapping and calling my name. My head pops up in a flash. Now Lee's driving. "Look Coco!" she yells. The sun makes it hard for my eyes to open wide, but I see trees and grass with a lot of colors and cars everywhere. Lee stops the car. Aunt Jean and Aunt Joyce take me for a walk by the trees. They have happy faces. My tail is happy too. All those trees to mark! I want everyone to know a new dog is in town!

STARTING OVER AGAIN

For a moment, I couldn't believe we had arrived! We thanked God for a safe journey and began scouting out the necessary stores to hit. It seemed as though everything you wanted or needed was located on this one long stretch of highway: a medical building, a grocery store, a pharmacy, a gym, and even a garden center. Gas stations were everywhere! Everything was so conveniently located. I was getting so excited! I couldn't wait to start my new life.

Finding my apartment complex was easy. I took a right turn off the highway and, a mile or so later, we were there. The green landscape was lush and plentiful. The smell of pine needles mixed with the aroma of many colorful flowers welcomed us as we drove down the path leading to the complex. I parked the car in a guest parking spot, opened the windows, and sat quietly in the car for a while to take it all in. Joyce, Jean, and even Coco were admiring the sights. Finally, I leapt out of the car and entered the office building to retrieve the key to my apartment. The attendants greeted me warmly and welcomed me to the neighborhood.

I had requested a first-floor rental to avoid the steps when it was time to walk Coco; however, I didn't realize until I arrived that the building had basement apartments. Unfortunately, someone else lived below me. They cautioned me to be careful when letting Coco run through the house. I wasn't looking forward to that challenge. Bad habits are hard to break.

Nevertheless, we forged ahead. As I circled the driveway to pull the car into my designated parking space, I could see Coco in the rearview mirror wiggling like an overgrown worm. It was potty time!

Hurry, Lee! Gotta go! Gotta go! She gets my leash, and away we go. I can tell that Aunt Joyce and Aunt Jean want to walk me too, but Lee beats them to it. What a lucky guy!

My paws are sticking to the grass like the time they were sticking to the fluffy white stuff. I love playing this game! I pull Lee around like she's on a leash too—searching for my spot. Lee lets me smell around for a long time. When I finish my business, Lee picks me up, and we go to see our new home. Lee and I have moved around a lot since Grand Master left to go where humans go when they are good. Thinking about Grand Master makes me want to give her a hug.

I want to give her a hug until I see her running around the house with her face smiling from ear to ear, like when Big Fellow was around. Aunt Joyce and Aunt Jean are smiling too. Am I missing something? Big Fellow isn't here! We left him behind!

I loved my new place! It was even larger than I expected. The sight of it in the brochure was misleading. A nice-sized sitting room separated the two bedrooms—very similar to our previous house, only smaller. Neutral colors of beige and white splashed the walls of the kitchen, which was just the right size for intimate gatherings. My mind raced with so many wonderful ideas about how to decorate—a bright color here, a metal wall hanging over there. I couldn't wait to get started!

Joyce and Jean decided to shop for a few items while I got Coco settled. I needed some kitchen and bathroom essentials. My furniture was on its way, and I also needed some products to do a little house cleaning prior to the delivery. Everything in the apartment looked clean enough, but I wanted to do a little sanitizing before settling in. Assured the furniture would be delivered only a few hours after I arrived, I had no time to waste.

Joyce and Jean returned to the house carrying a big basket of housecleaning products. We quickly started wiping and spraying and sweeping and dusting. I wanted us to get everything cleaned before the movers arrived.

Perfect timing! The truck pulled up just as we finished cleaning. I was so happy that Joyce and Jean were here to help me get settled. At that moment, I felt so blessed to have the greatest sister in the world and a wonderful sister-friend who supported me no matter what.

It didn't take the men long to unload the truck. When we were satisfied that everything had been delivered—damage free—the men drove off. Joyce, Jean, and I worked until it started to get dark before taking a break. To my surprise, Coco stayed out of the way. Whenever he saw the men bringing in a piece of furniture, he would run to a corner in the kitchen for safety. I was happy to treat him with a cookie for being such a good boy. I even let him run through the house to get acquainted…ignoring the basement. After all, it was his home too!

I'd better stay out of the way. Too much is going on! I'm afraid the moving men will step on my paw if I get too close. I can't let that happen. Lee won't be able to take me for my walks! I'm just a dog, but who lives in a place that's not clean? Lee always cleans my cage! These ladies will clean the fur off my back if I'm in their way! I'll stay in my corner and keep my eyes on the two men coming in and out of the house. I want to be ready if Lee needs help.

The men leave. Aunt Joyce, Aunt Jean, and Lee are laughing and running around the house like crazy humans! Are they playing a game without me? I don't know what's going on, but I'm going to play the game too. I run after them until I can't run any more. My legs need to stop running. I love it when Aunt Joyce and Aunt Jean are around. They never get tired like Lee. Lee says they are going back home after we're all moved in. Maybe they'll stay!

When the sun came up, Aunt Joyce and Aunt Jean were gone. I miss them being around. (Lee misses them too. I can tell.) Ladies fussing over a pup like me is doggy heaven. But I'm not any old dog. I'm special. My heart belongs to Lee…only Lee.

The days were filled with decorating the house and running back and forth to department stores to get one thing or another. It seemed like I returned more items than I purchased. I had become obsessed with making sure colors matched and designs complemented each other. Creating a home Coco and I could enjoy was so important to me. Whenever thoughts of Henry not being there crept into my mind, I found even more tasks to tackle. I missed him, but I knew I had made the right decision. I could not have lived with myself if I had compromised my values. Besides, I learned a long time ago that what is meant to be will be. So I decided not to spend my time pining for what was lost and to move on with my life, giving it all to God. I was pleased with how much I had grown.

It had been years since I lived in an apartment. Not sure I could have done it again if I hadn't had Coco. It was strange how a surprise birthday gift for Cliff had become a most cherished gift for me. Coco had become my family. He needed me, and I surely needed him, especially on this part of my life's journey. I couldn't imagine being without him. I thanked God every day for blessing me with such companionship. We were a package deal!

Cliff had been on my mind frequently since moving into my new place. I remembered the good times we had traveling. New York City was our favorite getaway. We both loved the hustle and bustle of the city and the city lights. We walked the streets until late in the night, people watching and sightseeing. I ate my first Belgian waffle in New York City—at the Sheraton. It was as light and fluffy as it was huge. What a treat that was! Best of all was going to the theatre. There's absolutely no place with a theatre district like New York City. Cliff and I never visited the city without seeing a musical. My all-time favorite is *Phantom of the Opera.* (I've seen it four times!) I missed Cliff's laughter and his adventurous spirit.

Without Cliff, and now Henry, I was beginning to feel a little melancholy. For a long time after Cliff died, I was angry about being left alone. My life had been so busy working and taking care of him. I had so many regrets and feelings of guilt. His death left a void in my life that could only be filled with tears of sorrow and grief. For so long, I needed and prayed for answers to so many questions: Why did he die so young? Did I do all that needed to be done to take care of him? Would I ever be happy again? How could I have been a better wife?

Henry had been an answer to my prayer to be able to feel something special for another man. At first, I wasn't concerned about getting married again, but I wanted companionship. I quickly learned that companionship comes with a cost—one that I was uncomfortable paying without marriage.

The good news is, all of my sorrows led me to a desire to have an authentic and loving relationship with Jesus Christ. With the help of my pastor, good friends who were spiritually grounded, and my desire to better understand the teachings of the Bible, I was eager to start a new life. I was so grateful to have Coco along for the journey.

I had been so busy moving that I had not thought too much about the affect these changes might have on Coco. Coco was such a happy, playful dog. He loved to play with adults more than children or other dogs. Although he wanted to go with me whenever I left the house, it was not always possible. Now that things were more settled, I could spend more time with him. I wanted to make it a priority.

Coco had not had a seizure in a very long time. The vet suggested a few years ago that I stop giving him his seizure medicine to see if he had outgrown the condition, though he warned me the condition could return, especially if Coco were stressed or sick with another illness. I hadn't thought about him having seizures until, a few weeks after our move, I found Coco dazed and lying on his side on the kitchen floor. I took him to a vet in the area, who advised me to put him back on his seizure medication. Fortunately, I had researched a vet for Coco and a primary-care physician for me shortly after we moved into the apartment. I was happy to have found a highly respected vet who could help care for him. Coco was my precious baby boy!

When Lee's gone, I look around and smell around the house—when I'm not taking a nap. She always comes back home with a lot of bags. When the sun comes up, Lee wakes up before me. She pats my head, rubs my belly, and gives me my peanut butter treat. She used to give me peanut butter treats a lot. (Wonder why she stopped?) Lee says what's inside the peanut butter will keep me strong. I love peanut butter treats, so I don't care what's inside. I don't need anything to make me strong. I am already strong! Sometimes, she gives me cheese balls. I like those too! Yummy, yummy!

When my food is gone, Lee takes me for a long walk. We always meet a new dog. I hate it when they try to smell me. Lee says they want to be my buddy. I don't need a new buddy. Big Fellow is my buddy. I don't like strange dogs getting too close to Lee. She needs me to protect her...and only me. (Grand Master left me in charge. I can't let him down!) When a dog gets too close to her, I bark and bark until Lee pulls me away by my leash. She loves that old leash.

"*Coco, you are the only dog barking. Why can't you be a good boy?*"

I stop barking but keep walking—with my head up, my tail wagging, and my mind on finding the next tree to mark. There's no time to be a good boy.

I get to ride with Lee when she goes in and out of the stores. She never likes taking me to the stores with food. She says I'd go crazy smelling all those cookies. I like it when Lee takes me with her to the window where you drive up. When the man behind the window sees my face, I know a treat's on the way. These doggy treats are smacking good! Sometimes Lee goes by the window and grabs some paper so fast, the man can't give me my treat. I'm not happy when that happens. I bark and bark until Lee finds a treat in the car.

Lee takes me riding to see the place she says is the big city! We see a lot of cars and big houses—so big I have to poke my head out the window and look up and up to see them (like the first time I met Big Fellow). We have a lot of fun. I'm starting to like this place. Lee is too. I can tell.

ONE HOME TOO MANY

Living in an apartment was fine for a while. It had only been three months, and I was already beginning to feel very uneasy about not knowing my neighbors. As soon as I thought I had made a new friend, in a few weeks, that person was gone. Nobody in my building, it seemed, stayed in their apartments longer than a few months. Walking Coco at night didn't feel safe anymore. If I had a problem, I didn't feel I could knock on my neighbor's door for help, like I could where I lived in upstate New York. It's so nice when you know all your neighbors. Here, I knew no one. Furthermore, the lady in the basement apartment below mine complained to management that we were making too much noise. Coco and I could hardly move without her knowing it. The floors and walls were paper thin. And forget about letting Coco run through the house: our chasing days were over. Coco made sure that I knew he was not a happy camper. Whenever he was in a rebellious mood, he would run through the house like a dog on wheels, until I cornered him and put him in his cage. Needless to say, this did not end well. Even after my neighbor and I agreed to work together to resolve—or at least minimize—the problem, I wasn't comfortable with the situation. I wanted Coco to be free to live in his own space. Several more weeks passed, and I decided it was time to look for a house.

Carol, my realtor, was a very patient and knowledgeable lady who did her best to address my needs. We immediately started looking at houses in and out of the area. I wanted to get an overview of the housing market and an understanding of the pros and cons of living in specific housing developments. I was surprised at the number of developments with amenities. Dog parks, pools, and walking trails were very popular, especially in locations with single-family dwellings. The grounds were beautifully landscaped with lots of pine trees and seasonal flowers. Spring was in the air, and many homeowners, or the landscapers, were busy mulching, planting, and watering to beautify their lawns. There were so many lovely houses to choose from. But, as God had guided me many times before, I was sure He would lead me to the right home for me and Coco. I needed to be patient.

Lee goes out a lot with some lady. Lee said they are house hunting. I don't know, but it's strange to me. Why go hunting for another house when you already have one? Something's up. I don't like it when Lee leaves me here alone so long. I have a plan: I'll run to the door and play dead when Lee comes back. Maybe if Lee thinks I'm dead, she'll stay home.

When I hear the lady's car, I run to the door before Lee can come in. I lie down in front of the door so she won't be able to open it without moving me out of the way. I wait...and wait...and wait, until I fall asleep. I wake up when I hear Lee at the front door. This time, playing dead is the last thing on my mind. I want to go out to look for the closest tree. (An accident is on the way!) Lee forgot it was time to take me for my walk. She comes in saying something about how she lost her key and couldn't get into the apartment. She went to the office to get another key. (But what about my plan?) I start running around in circles like a mad dog until Lee stops talking. (A dog's gotta go when a dog's gotta go!)

"I'm sorry, Coco," she said, "let's go!"

We walk fast so I can find my spot before it's too late. Lee keeps talking, but I'm not listening. I'm circling and smelling for the sweet spot. (Oh, what a relief!) When we get home, Lee kicks off her shoes and lies down on the big chair. Guess our little walk tired her out. I get on the floor with my head resting on her feet, ready to hear all about her day.

Lee talks and talks. I don't hear much. No matter how hard I try, I can't keep my eyes open. This old dog is losing his steam. My eyes are almost closed, but when I see that Lee is about to put me into my crate, my old eyes pop wide open. (Not the crate!) I guess the look on my face surprises Lee, so she lets me snooze in my favorite corner in the house—where I can keep one eye on her.

Lee starts walking all around the house. I can tell she's worried. She stops to pick up a crumb on the floor near my bowl. She wipes the food table. Lee finds work to do to stop her from worrying. (I don't understand humans! Why worry when you can sleep on it?)

It was settled! I hadn't planned on moving so soon. My goal was to stay in the apartment for at least a year to give me time to decide if this part of Charlotte was where I wanted to make my permanent home. But I was feeling more uneasy as time passed. I knew I could not last a year in the apartment. I asked God to please give me a sign. He did. After six months, the leasing department decided to raise my rent from the promotional fee to an increased fee for the rest of the term. That fee was as much as the mortgage payment for my last house!

Carol and I had been looking at homes for a while, so I knew I had a few options. Unfortunately, her first choice was a rather new development across the state line in South Carolina. She insisted that the area was going to be a hot spot in a few years. I wasn't convinced, but I decided to follow her lead. Surely she knew more than I did about those matters.

I still wrestled with the idea of living in South Carolina. As a child who grew up in the South during the Jim Crow era, South Carolina was a place that brought back memories of racial problems and segregation pitfalls. Stories of lynching and other injustices soured my appetite for southern living—especially in places like South Carolina, Georgia, Mississippi, and Alabama. Those areas had the greatest reputations for Whites refusing to accept Black people living in their neighborhoods. How could I call any of those places home?

Friends of mine helped me see that change would only happen in those states if more Blacks and other people of color lived there to help alter the landscape and the political atmosphere. I wasn't an activist by any means, yet I was certainly open to learning more about how to support a *new south,* a term others used to describe the migration taking place at the time. All things considered, I decided to think positive thoughts about relocating to South Carolina. I put a deposit down to begin building a cute little ranch in a development situated across the North Carolina–South Carolina State line. It had enough yard space for Coco to run free.

Whenever Lee picks me up and starts playing with my ears, I know something's up!

"Coco, we are getting a new home. It will be a place where you can run and play with other dogs. You won't have to worry about anyone complaining about the noise you make when running through the house. It will be great!" Lee says without stopping to breathe.

I'm surprised! (What's she talking about...another home? We just moved here! I'm a pretty easygoing fellow, but enough is enough!) I open my big eyes as wide as I can and look at Lee's eyes without a blink. I hope she can read my mind. (Because If I could really talk, I would tell her how I really felt about moving to another house. And it wouldn't be pretty!) Maybe I'm missing something. Maybe Lee is having that breakdown many humans talk about. Poor girl, she has been through so much. Maybe she's at the end of her leash. Thinking about it makes my stomach do flips.

"It's okay, Coco." (Guess she read my mind.) "Trust me. You will love our new home." I'm not happy about moving again. Can't Lee tell? I'm getting older, and my legs can't stretch like before. I can't walk a long time or jump steps. I hope there're no steps in this new home!

CROSSING STATE LINES

Lee is full of surprises. Before, she said she never wanted to move south. She said Jim Crow made it hard for her growing up. Because of someone named Jim Crow, Lee couldn't sit in the front of the bus. I'm confused. How can anyone keep you from sitting where you want to sit? Maybe the seat belonged to someone else. Lee says the South is still listening to Mr. Crow instead of Dr. King. Thanks to Dr. King, she can sit in the front of the bus, not the back of the bus. This "back of the bus" and "Mr. Jim Crow" and "Dr. King" talk is too much for my doggy ears. This had better be our last move. I don't think this old body can take moving again.

Four months later, the new house was ready for us to move in. Settling into a new home is always a challenge, but this move was even more so. I practically had to do it alone. Because of a change in my closing date, the two friends who had volunteered to help me move were unavailable. I figured it was too late to ask anyone else to help me on such short notice. I was a bundle of nerves, but I had to move forward. Arrangements had already been made for the movers to transport the big stuff, but I had too many boxes to move by myself! But "can't" was not an option. After closing on the house, the realtor handed me the keys to the house and…game on!

Buoyed by a mixture of excitement and fear, I raced to my car (I thanked God it was an SUV.), drove frantically to the apartment, and started loading up. I was also grateful that my new house was only minutes away from the apartment. Loading and unloading, I drove back and forth from the apartment to the house, taking only boxes I was strong enough to lift. I had no idea how I would get the heavier boxes moved, but I refused to think about it. I knew God would make a way.

Lee is running back and forth from house to the house like a crazy woman, stepping over my cute little feet as she moves about. I circle around her feet, smelling boxes and tugging on her shoelaces. (I love shoelaces!) Lee stops to play with me for a while. But I can tell her heart's not in it. I don't care about all this moving around. I don't give a dog's bone how she feels! I nip at her shoelaces until she trips over me.

"Coco!" she says in a loud voice, like she's had enough of me. "Get back! You're going to hurt us both!" Lee goes out the door with another box.

That's enough to send me to my corner with my tail tucked between my legs. It's not like Lee to leave without giving me a pat on the head. I know to stay in my corner until she comes back for the next box.

When Lee comes back to get more boxes, she's not alone. She's with two men. She tells them my name. They look at me and look at each other. Lee tells me the two men are there to help her move the boxes. Looks like they can't hear. They don't seem to know what she's saying. They just look at each other. Lee starts talking to them with her hands. Watching Lee play with her hands makes me want to play that game. Maybe if I wiggle my tail, they'll hear me too!

I knew God had my back. The two men who had been at the new house painting all day were just finishing up. They had been trying to complete the painting before I was scheduled to move in, but they were running behind on all of their jobs. The men were starting to do cleanup when I returned with another load of boxes. (The thought of them hanging around the house long past their quitting time—while I was still moving boxes! Only God!) I was hesitant to ask for their help, especially since they had been working all day. Surely, they were eager to get home. But I was desperate. Since neither of the men spoke English, I struggled to communicate my need for their help. Fortunately, I was able to convey that I needed help moving boxes, and that I would pay them for their assistance.

The white van the painters were driving was loaded with paint, ladders, and tools, leaving limited space to move all of the boxes in one trip. So we made several trips to complete the job. I thanked them, and I thanked God. Sending those two men to help me was a lifesaver and a blessing!

By nightfall, everything had been moved out of the apartment and put in its proper place in our new home. Coco was the last one to be transported. When I made that last trip to get him, I literally fell on the bare floor and rested there for a long time before I could move again. I guess Coco thought I had fallen asleep. He slid over next to me and put his wet, cold nose under my chin to rouse me. I pulled him even closer to me and gave him a big hug. I hoped he knew I was sorry for yelling at him earlier. After holding on to him for a while, I whispered softly in his ear, "Let's go home."

ONE DOG TOO MANY

Lee puts my leash on my collar, smiles at me, and tickles me behind the ears. She's so happy to get me out for a walk at our new home. I can tell. She says the walking trail is big with lots of grass. (And so many mailboxes to mark!) My tail is wagging just thinking about the fun I'll have playing games.

"We are home for the last time," she whispers as we walk.

That's music to my doggy ears! I'm tired of moving around. Change is hard for an old dog like me. We're set in our ways and move a lot slower.

Getting used to this new house won't be easy. I see steps at the porch! How do I get to the walking trail? I stop and stand there for a long time. Lee pulls my leash as she walks down the steps.

"Come on, Coco. You can do it!"

"Oh no, I can't!" I bark, looking up like she's lost her mind. I'm getting too old for steps.

Makes me think of that fall when Lee thought I was hurt. I break out into a doggy sweat thinking about it. It happened at our old house before we moved south. On one of our walks, Lee stopped to see this house that nobody lived in. She went in, holding on to my leash. I pulled on my leash, walked in front of her, and fell down a big hole. When Lee looked down at me, her face looked sick. Yelling my name, she climbed down the steps on the wall and grabbed me. Lee held me so close. I could feel her heart making noise as I snuggled into her arms. But I was okay. Fast on my feet, I landed on my feet, not my head. I coulda been a goner!

I guess Lee forgot about my fall or she wouldn't be waiting for me to jump down those steps! She tugs and tugs on my leash. I stay. (I'm not moving.) She walks back up the steps, picks me up, walks me down the steps, and places my feet on the ground. (That was one battle I was going to win!)

I keep my head up, and Lee follows. When we walk to the grassy spot, a lady comes over to walk with us—with her little mutt! Then another lady comes over to walk her dog. The grassy hill is full of dogs and ladies! We dogs smell and push each other around, and the ladies talk a lot.

I've had enough! I bark like a crazy dog and pull on my leash so hard that Lee stumbles—about to fall to the ground. I keep pulling and barking until we reach the house. Lee walks behind me. She's not happy. (I couldn't stand one more dog smelling me. I guess I lost it!) She picks me up, walks me up the steps, and leads me into the house. The house is quiet until it's time for my nap. (Not off to a good start. Living in our old house didn't seem so bad after all.)

When the sun comes up, Lee is back to her lovable self. We have fun playing on our walk—no ladies, no dogs. Then she gives me the old "Why can't you play with the other dogs?" talk as we walk. I close my ears and keep walking. I like it when it's just me and Lee.

I was amazed at how fast time had flown by. Almost four months had passed since Coco and I moved into our new home. It felt like yesterday! I was delighted that Joyce was coming for a short visit. I wanted her to be our first guest. After all, she would always have a room there whenever she needed a break from the West Coast. Joyce and Coco had developed a special bond. He loved her almost as much as I did. And I knew she loved him too.

One morning while Joyce was getting dressed for the day, Coco snuck into her bedroom. Ready to play, he started pulling on one end of her bra, which had slipped out of Joyce's hand as she was trying to snap it on. Coco must have thought Joyce was teaching him how to play a new game. He sunk his teeth into the end of her bra that had slipped out of her hand and started pulling. Joyce was laughing so hard while trying to pull the bra from Coco's clutches, she must have broken his concentration. He let go and stared at her like he was confused about what had happened. Joyce and I both couldn't stop laughing.

We had a great time showing Joyce all the new sights in the Carolinas. She was astounded at how much the South had changed since our childhood. Neither of us had spent too much time exploring the South since we moved away. Joyce promised her next trip would be longer.

It's always playtime when Aunt Joyce is in the house. I love it when Aunt Joyce drops food from her plate (like Grand Master). I watch that floor like a hawk—the good food again! Not one crumb of the good food gets past me. She always gives me that look: "That's our little secret. Don't you say a word!"

Aunt Joyce likes to play games with me. Sometimes she throws one of Lee's bedroom shoes for me to catch. I'm a little slow moving, but once I catch on to the game, I'm a winner. I run after that shoe and get it back to Aunt Joyce so fast, she can't throw it back fast enough! We have a lot of fun playing tug of war. Aunt Joyce grabs one end of that same shoe, and I sink my teeth into the other end. We pull and pull until Aunt Joyce lets go. I hold on so tight, she says she's afraid I will pull my teeth out trying to be the alpha dog. Can't say she's wrong. I'm in it to win it all the way! Nobody plays the pulling game like Aunt Joyce!

I think Lee knows how much fun I have with Aunt Joyce and wants to play games with us too. (I hope she's not thinking I like Aunt Joyce more than her.) Lee and Aunt Joyce like it when I grab Lee's shoe and run around the house like a mad dog. They run after me but can't catch me. They come close when I have to slow down for that table with the four sharp corners that Lee says can hurt me. I always slow down—afraid I'll go headfirst into one of those sharp corners, and it'll be my last run. I can see the headlines now: Mad dog becomes a dead dog. He knocked himself out!

GUESS WHO'S COMING TO DINNER...AGAIN

I was surprised at how fast Coco and I adjusted to our new home. Everyone in the neighborhood was so nice. We even had neighbors with dogs who wanted to walk with us. Coco liked it better when we walked alone, but I wanted him to have some playmates, so I continued to drag him along.

We enjoyed our routine rides around the community, searching for grocery stores, drug stores, pet stores, and other specialty shops we would need. Coco was glued to his favorite spot, perched on the window ledge on the passenger side, as he took in all the sights. Though most places we traveled were in North Carolina, South Carolina was not so bad after all.

In 2010, when Coco and I moved to my new house, Barack Obama was still president. It seemed everyone went out of their way to be more accepting and more tolerant of one another during his presidency. Surprisingly, I saw very few Confederate flags, which were known to flood the southern states. Most unexpectedly were the number of people of color who held professional jobs:

dentists, pharmacists, physicians, and more. Slowly, my misconceptions of the South were fading and giving way to a new attitude about the progress that had been made since I left my hometown and moved up North. White people were more friendly—in a genuine way, not that stereotypical *southern-hospitality* way. The South was always known for its welcoming manner, but those of us who grew up there knew that the kindness shown was only intended to go so far. You still needed to remember *your place.*

While I was busy settling into my new life, one night—out of the blue—Henry called. I was shocked. I hadn't heard from him since I left New York. He said he wanted to talk about renewing our relationship. It didn't take long for us to realize that we still loved each other and wanted to be together. So we agreed to spend time together, talk through our differences, and decide the direction of our future.

We had many conversations over the phone before we decided to see each other. Weeks passed. Finally, I felt the time was right. When Henry asked if he could come for a visit, I readily agreed. I couldn't wait to see him again!

Big Fellow and Lee are playing the dating game again! Lee said he's coming for a visit. I'm confused. Why would Lee want to play the dating game with someone she had moved so far to get away from? Maybe dogs aren't supposed to know, but I'm "bamboozled." (I heard that word somewhere. I like it!) Maybe she's forgotten the times I snuggled with her and lapped her wet face and nose—ugh! I can't understand why I'm not enough for her. I'm going to my doggy bed. Maybe everything will be better when the sun comes up.

Big Fellow is here! It's like old times! When he walks through the door, I stop and look, not wanting to be so friendly this time around. (What if he leaves again?) "What the heck!" I take off—running around the table with the four sharp corners like before. Big Fellow is not far behind. (I guess he missed me too.)

"You've still got it!" he said while trying to catch his breath. "I thought you would be too old for this!"

Whew! If he only knew! We start breathing fast, trying to get enough air as we flop on the floor. My chest is beating like a drum. Big Fellow picks me up, cradles me in his long arms, and rubs me all over with his big hands. (Like old times!) I'm sure everything will work out just fine this time with Big Fellow, Lee, and me!

Lee and Big Fellow are having what Lee calls a long-distance relationship. I guess that means she goes a long way to see him, and I stay home. When Lee sees Big Fellow long distance, she takes me to a nice place she calls the doggy hotel—but not like Puppy Paradise. She told the ladies who take care of me that I'm her special baby boy. (I like that!) I don't want Lee to know, but sometimes when I'm at the doggy hotel my belly aches and flips over inside. I don't want her to worry. It goes away when it's playtime.

The ladies love me and play with me whenever I want to play. (A cute little pup keeps her eyes on me.) The other dogs like to play with me too. They don't smell me like the dogs on the walking trail at home. (I hate that!) These dogs like to run and play with the balls in the yard. We run around each other all day until the ladies give us our treats. They take us to our cages, and it's nap time!

WEDDING BELLS—AT LAST

After almost seven years of an on-again, off-again romance, Henry and I agreed it was time to recommit and get married. We understood the work involved in building a successful relationship. Spending time apart had given us the opportunity to assess what we wanted for our future and what we needed from each other. We were ready to say, "I do!"

Henry would be able to retire in 2013. So we decided to get married the summer before his retirement and continue our commute back and forth until all plans had been completed for him to relocate. We spent many hours talking about whether or not to have a wedding. Neither of us wanted a big wedding, but we wanted to share our special day with members of our family in some way. We both knew how expensive a wedding could be and planned to save money to purchase another house at some point. It was important for us to eventually buy a home together—one with more space—to accommodate both of our belongings and to have room for family to visit when possible. However, we vowed to wait until we were sure we could handle it financially. (I had learned a thing or two when married to Cliff about getting into debt too soon; I was not about to make the same mistake.)

It wasn't until we sat down to compile the guest list that we realized how difficult it was to make a decision. By the time we listed everyone who was important to us, we realized it wouldn't be wise to have a wedding and be unable to accommodate all our family and friends. Henry's family alone would fill a small chapel, not to mention extended family and friends. My list was shorter, but not nearly short enough to justify spending the big bucks it would take to celebrate in style. There were too many people whom we couldn't bear to leave out, yet planning a wedding to include everyone on our guest list would sink our budget.

There was also the question of where to hold the wedding. Having a wedding in the Carolinas would require traveling expenses for most of our friends and family. It didn't seem like a good time to ask them to make such a sacrifice. The economy was suffering from the bank failure disaster, and some loved ones had lost their jobs or were starting new ones. We didn't want anyone to feel obligated to attend our wedding, especially if it were a financial struggle.

Since both of us had been married before, neither one of us felt strongly about planning another wedding. We thought a private ceremony would address any disappointment uninvited guests would have about not being able to witness the occasion. So we made peace with having a private ceremony—a private ceremony in a church.

*Picture me walking with Lee to give her to Big Fellow! Lee said her
father went to that place where humans go when they have been
good, like Grand Master. She said he can't give her to Big Fellow. I
don't like giving Lee to anybody. I want to keep her! Why give her
away? (I don't want Lee to give me away.) And why be happy about
giving Lee to a man who let her leave him? I like Big Fellow a lot,
but what if he lets her leave him again? All this giving-away talk
makes no sense to me. I hope Lee's not planning to give me away!*

*Lee is so happy now. She was so sad for a long time when Grand
Master left. I'm going to keep my eye on this one. If he hurts Lee, he'll
have to answer to me. Why didn't I chew his shoes when I had the
chance? (The sight of me with that great big shoe makes me giggle.
I couldn't chew that big shoe apart for all the cookies in doggy land.
And everybody knows how much I love cookies!)*

Henry and I were satisfied that we had finally settled on a private
wedding ceremony. The next task was deciding where to have it.
I really wanted to get married in a church. But which church?
Even though I had joined a church in Charlotte, I hadn't been a
member long enough to get well acquainted with the pastor. It
was a much bigger church than I was used to, and I was having a
difficult time fitting in. And Henry had visited only a few times.
I didn't care about not having a traditional wedding, but I was
definitive about exchanging vows administered by a member of
the clergy who knew us as a couple.

Our former pastor, Pastor Ford, the one who had appointed
us stewards of our church in New York, was now the senior pastor of a church in a town nearby. He had been reassigned to this

new church a few years before I relocated to the Carolinas. Henry and I had met and starting dating as members of his church in New York. Since I didn't believe in coincidences, I was sure this was divine intervention! Once again, God had my back! It was settled: Henry and I would ask our former pastor to perform the wedding ceremony in his church. He gladly agreed.

We would exchange wedding vows privately in the church of our beloved pastor and friend, Pastor Ford. Henry's son, Mark, and my sister, Joyce, would be witnesses. My friend, Reverend Terry, would pray a special blessing, and my friend Jean's husband, Cleave, would sing a special wedding tribute. There would be no other guests invited. It was a wrap!

BEST-LAID PLANS

Looks like I won't have to be give Lee to Big Fellow after all! Boy! Am I happy about that! The sad part is, I won't be at the wedding. Lee and Big Fellow are having a wedding with no people—just Big Fellow and Lee. Why would two people in love, who waited so long to have a wedding, have a wedding with no people? Sounds a little crazy to me, but what do I know? I'm just a dog! Lee is full of surprises. I wonder how long I'll be at the doggy hotel with those ladies. Maybe that cute little pup with the bow in her hair will be waiting for me!

June 12, 2012—my wedding day was finally here! There was an unusual calmness in the air, not the hustle and bustle that accompany most weddings. I insisted on cooking breakfast for my guests. After breakfast, everyone busied themselves getting ready for the big moment. Joyce and I had organized my wedding attire the night before. I decided to get dressed at the church to avoid damage to my beautiful dress. Joyce made sure everything I needed was packed and ready to be given to me once we reached the church. Even though the church destination was an hour and a half drive, everyone else decided it would be best to dress at the house, instead of the church, to simplify matters.

Jean and her husband, Cleave, arrived at the house, signaling it was time for us to get on the highway. Reverend Terry, who lived a few hours away, was expected to meet everyone at the church. As the wedding party gathered outside, Henry instructed Jean and Cleave to follow our car to the church. I sat in the front with Henry, and Joyce, her husband Ron, and Mark sat in the back. Mark has a sense of humor like his dad. He kept us laughing along the way.

The trip to the church was uneventful. Traffic was not too heavy for a Saturday afternoon, and we arrived on time at approximately two o'clock. The ceremony was scheduled for four o'clock. Pastor Ford was waiting for us at the side door entrance of the church near the church parking lot. Reverend Terry was already there and was inside with Pastor Ford's wife, Marilyn. As we proceeded to gather our belongings from the cars before entering the church, I didn't see the garment bag containing the wedding dress.

"Where is my dress?"

"The dress? Oh, the dress…Don't you have it? I thought you had it!" Aunt Joyce responded in a panic.

"No, I thought you had it," I answered, trying to remain calm.

Everyone stopped what they were doing and looked in disbelief toward me and Joyce. The dress was missing! We all stood still—in silence—in shock!

"We can get married without the dress," Henry blurted out, trying to ease the tension.

Joyce burst into tears. "I'm sorry. I thought you had the dress. I didn't see it hanging where we left it last night."

"Don't worry about it." I could see how distraught Joyce was, and I didn't want her to blame herself for an obvious mistake. Seeing her so upset was breaking my heart. It had been a very long time since I had seen my sister cry. She was usually not a crier.

While I was comforting Joyce, Mark, who had retrieved the keys from his dad, was headed toward the car.

"I'm going back to get the dress."

"I'm going with you," Joyce yelled, trying to hold back the tears.

By this time, my sister was almost inconsolable. I was holding her hand and trying to reassure her everything would be okay.

"I'm okay," Joyce insisted, calming herself while pulling away from me to join Mark in the car. They drove off in a flash!

"Be safe," I yelled. "Don't drive too fast."

As they drove off, everyone walked wearily toward the side entrance of the church. Jean grabbed my hand to console me as the pastor invited us to come in and relax. He assured Henry and me that it would all work out. Fortunately, Pastor Ford didn't have another commitment for the day and was prepared to wait for the dress. At that moment, I was grateful that we were having a private ceremony.

While everyone waited, I tried to keep myself busy. The ladies tried to engage me in small talk to keep me from thinking about what had happened. Henry, Cleave, and Ron had gathered in the pastor's study while the ladies were socializing in one of the pastor's conference rooms. Since Joyce wasn't there to help me, I excused myself from the group to go to the ladies' room to style my hair. Jean rushed over to follow me, but I insisted I could do it alone.

I tried to block out the sound of chatter coming from the other rooms—I just wanted silence. I needed to hear from God. I needed His reassurance that everything would work out. Looking in the mirror, I tried to put my beautiful hair pin of white pearls and crystal lace in the right position in my hair. My fingers wouldn't let me complete the task. Staring blankly at the mirror, I waited for the tears to come. They never did. I stayed in the ladies' room so long, Henry was worried and came in to check on me.

"Are you okay, Sweetie Pie? Everything's going to be fine." Sweetie Pie was our name for each other when we were being affectionately playful—Henry's way of trying to cheer me up.

I assured him I was okay. Henry realized that I didn't want him to see me crying, so he reluctantly gave me the space I needed to keep from falling apart.

"Call me if you need me. I'm going back to talk noise with the fellows."

"I won't be much longer," I managed to say calmly. Henry was trying very hard to minimize the tension in the air. I didn't want him to worry about me.

Honestly, I left the room so the others wouldn't see me cry. I was hurting, not because of the dress, but because I knew the pain Joyce was feeling. I had never seen her so upset. I even called her a couple times, just to check on her. But she didn't answer. *Too busy crying,* I thought. She probably felt that she had let me down. I didn't want her to feel that way. Mistakes happen. But I could only imagine how I would have felt if the roles were reversed. I felt so sad for Joyce. We were so close, and I loved her so much. Frankly, I was more concerned about Joyce than a wedding dress. For that reason, I was especially grateful that Mark was willing to go back to get the dress. I knew having that dress would be the only way Joyce could begin to forgive herself.

In the meantime, I busied myself fussing with my hair, when I wasn't gazing out of the window. Soon, Jean came in to check on me. I assured her that I was okay. I told her I needed to be alone to calm my nerves. She understood. Jean was such a faithful friend and a fixer. I knew it was killing her not to be able to solve this problem.

It was getting close to three thirty when I heard a car pulling into the church parking lot. I could see the car from the bathroom window. *That didn't take long*, I thought with a slight grin on my face—a weight had been lifted. I hurried back to where the ladies had gathered. Joyce and I hugged each other tearfully as I continued to reassure her that everything was fine.

Dress saga now resolved, Pastor Ford led the others into the sanctuary while Joyce helped me get dressed. She combed my hair in place before adorning it with the beautifully decorated hair pin: something new. My dress was a perfect fit. Joyce handed me a lovely bouquet of red roses adorned with white lace and a white bow. "You look beautiful," she whispered. For the first time in a long time, I felt beautiful!

To my delight and surprise, my beloved Pastor Ford and his wife had planned a traditional wedding ceremony with music, flowers, candles, the works—everything except wedding guests. The sanctuary looked so festive, and I was beaming with joy. Everyone was in place. Henry was standing up front next to Pastor Ford as I entered the room. Walking slowly down the aisle, my eyes met his eyes. He looked handsome in his dark-blue suit and his matching striped tie. He was standing tall with Mark by his side. He smiled. I smiled back.

The ceremony was simple but touching. The candle-lighting ritual and the communion service added special meaning to a special day. Joyce and I were in tears during the exchange of vows. This time, they were tears of joy. Everything had, indeed, worked out fine.

A FAMILIAR "MAN OF THE HOUSE"

Henry and I were finally married! I was elated. It was a bit surreal, since both of us were somewhat anxious about the responsibility of wedlock. The unanswered question was: Could we get past the walls that had kept us emotionally safe to become vulnerable again? Henry and I were sensitive souls who hurt easily. It would take time, but we were up for the challenge. The one thing we were both sure of was that we wanted to spend the rest of our lives together.

Since we had agreed to live apart and travel back and forth to see each other until Henry retired, we had a short honeymoon. Henry needed to get back to work. In many ways, these trips and our reunions were so exciting. We looked forward to seeing each other and spent hours talking about what we wanted our future to look like: our home, our travels, our hopes, our dreams. We had decided prior to our wedding that we would live for a while in our present home in South Carolina. Doing so would allow us more time to determine if we wanted to remain in South Carolina permanently. Before getting married, we considered moving to other locations, such as communities outside of Atlanta. However, I had grown fond of the Carolinas. My desire to relocate had waned. After all, living in the Carolinas had many benefits: close to the mountains, close to great beaches, and short drives to interesting places like Florida, Charleston, even Atlanta. Most of all, staying put for a while would give us more time to adjust to being married before making a major decision. Although our path to matrimony was quite a journey, I was happy to be Mrs. Henry Stuart III. It felt good. And yes, I was ready to have this man in the house!

I like having Big Fellow around the house. He still likes me, I can tell. He likes running after me all around the house, and I like to run. Sometimes Lee joins the fun. The two of them run after me from one end of the house to the other. I like when they run around in circles trying to get me. (Two grown-ups running after one cute little pooch—catch me if you can! It never happens!)

The hardest thing is trying not to fall over Big Fellow's big shoes. Lee said no running with shoes on, but sometimes he leaves them in our way. One time, Lee almost hit the floor trying to get around those shoes. I won't forget the look on her face.

"I'm sorry," Big Fellow said. "I'll be more careful where I put my shoes next time."

I'm not so sure about that...looks like I saw a smile on his face as he walked away. The good thing is Lee is happy. I see the look in her eyes like when Grand Master was around. She plays with me a lot. I love it when we play with her shoe with hair like mine all around it. One time, I grabbed her shoe, and Lee wouldn't let go. She was tugging as hard as she could, but my teeth were dug in! I pulled Lee's shoe so hard, she almost fell...again!

"Coco, turn it loose!" Big Fellow yelled. "Someone could get hurt."

"And that would be you," I wanted to bark back, but I stopped playing the game and sat down. Big Fellow never yelled at me before. I wasn't pleased! Grand Master only did it a few times. But he was Grand Master. Big Fellow hadn't been there long enough to yell at me. He was not Grand Master. I raised my head up high enough to look in his eyes with my big eyes wide open, I looked for a long time. Big Fellow reached down to rub my head, but I walked away with my tail straight up and found my favorite spot. It was time to take a nap before someone got hurt. When I woke up from my nap (I'd had a chance to sleep on it), Big Fellow and I were best buds again!

Our year apart passed quickly, and Henry had moved in full time. He and Coco were getting along just great. I knew Coco could be a handful at times, and he was very protective of me. I wasn't sure why I was so worried, since Henry had doggy-sat many times while we were dating in upstate New York. But things were different now. We were a family, and I wanted Henry to feel at home in our home. I knew it bothered him to live in a house that we had not purchased together. He told me so. I needed him to get past that notion and relax, knowing what was mine was his, and what was his was mine. At least that was the way I felt.

But that would take some time. I confess, I still struggled with sharing, especially the bathroom. I was passionate about keeping things neat, clean, and organized (some would say almost to an obsessive-compulsive degree). Achieving those goals was a lot easier living alone. At first, I found myself cleaning nonstop until I realized how impractical that was—not to mention how tiring it became.

Before Henry and I married, I actually hired a cleaning lady to help with house chores. It was a luxury that I convinced myself I not only wanted but needed to keep me sane. I could afford to treat myself. It didn't take long to find out that good cleaning help was hard to maintain. So I decided to save myself the headache of constantly seeking new help and do the cleaning myself.

Henry and I willingly shared household chores: cooking, cleaning, grocery shopping, walking Coco, taking out the garbage, etc. I was delighted! I had grown so tired of doing things on my own and by myself. I loved having a man to share these duties with. Unlike a lot of men, Henry did not seem to mind at all. I loved him even more for it. Furthermore, he was such a handyman. Fixing and repairing items around the house was a breeze for him. Henry seemed pleased when he could make repairs himself, rather than hire someone.

We both needed our space at times, so we were tuned in when one of us slipped away to another room to be alone. I realized that Henry had a lot to adjust to: retirement, relocation, marriage, a new home, a family. I, on the other hand, had succeeded in getting past some of those milestones and was ready for the next level. It didn't take me too long to understand that I needed to slow down and let time do what time does—grow patience and wisdom.

My biggest adjustment was settling into a big family again. Henry was one of seven brothers, two sisters, and several aunts and uncles. They were all very close and enjoyed spending time together. I had very little experience with family gatherings. Reunions and family visits were rare in my family. Generally, I was the one doing the visiting, except for Joyce. It had always been me and Joyce since we left the big house and graduated college. We visited each other whenever we had an opportunity.

Everyone in the family knew that Joyce and I had a special bond that had developed when we were kids. We were only eighteen months apart, and even though I was older, growing up together in the big house, we felt like twins—one chocolate and one vanilla, some commented. Joyce has a very fair complexion, and my skin is much darker. We knew the stigma around skin color, but it never interfered with our relationship. We loved each other just the way we were. There were times during our early childhood that I felt jealous of the attention Joyce received because of her skin color, but she never made me feel inferior. In fact, she often talked about how our teachers thought I was the smart one. We were always there to support each other, no matter the circumstances. We followed in each other's footsteps, secretly competing along the way. That's how close we were.

Henry had a great relationship with Joyce from the start and encouraged us to continue spending time with each other as usual. But he only had to adjust to one person. We had other brothers and sisters, but Joyce and I were inseparable. The only sibling who didn't live in Detroit, Henry was intentional about staying in touch with each family member who was still there. He enjoyed visiting Detroit and looked forward to his family visiting us. Knowing how he felt about his family, I was eager to be embraced by them. Upon meeting each one for the first time,

I discovered my worrying was not necessary. Everyone welcomed me and made me feel right at home.

It didn't take long to see that our families had more in common than we envisioned. His family had a few jokesters, and so did mine. His family had to struggle through some very difficult times to survive, and so did mine. Soon, I genuinely looked forward to visiting Detroit and was excited when any of his family members planned their vacations with us.

My one regret was not being able to take Coco on long trips. Flying was out of the question. We had a very bad experience with air travel when Cliff died. After his funeral, Coco and I flew to California to spend time with Joyce. I didn't want him to be alone. I was told Coco had to be medicated before flying because of the noise. I was assured he would be safe. Furthermore, I knew other dogs flew. I had seen them many times during my travels in the past, coming down the baggage transporter in their crates, their owners eagerly waiting to greet them. However, I did not know they were transported in the cargo section of the plane. I thought planes had a special section on the plane for pets, separate from cargo. With everything going on in my life, I had neglected to do my research. Coco was nauseous for days. I want to cry every time I think about what I put him through. Feeling enormously guilty, I promised Coco I would never put him on a flight again.

I avoided thinking about how Coco had aged since then. His whiskers were graying, and at his last appointment, the vet cautioned us to watch for signs of arthritis. He also seemed to be eating less—except for his favorite cookie treats. Even though Coco was almost fifteen years old (105 years old in dog years), he still had a lot of spunk. He loved running around the house, especially when we chased him. I didn't want to become a worrywart, but I knew I couldn't lose Coco. It would be too much.

I had no choice but to rely on the doggy hotel or his personal vet to keep him safe while Henry and I traveled. Having convinced myself that Coco was okay with the plan, I searched for the best location possible, regardless of the expense. I just wanted Coco to be well taken care of and have some fun with the other dogs.

I'm happy for Lee and this marriage thing, but I don't like going to another doggy hotel every time Big Fellow takes Lee away. They travel a lot! I don't like it! I don't want Lee to know, but sometimes, I don't eat my food at the doggy hotel. My belly rolls when I see the food coming. I try to eat so Lee won't worry about me. Sometimes, I eat, and it comes back out. Lee said when you get older, things are not the same. Guess I'm getting to be an old dog.

I like it when Lee and Big Fellow take me with them. They know how much I love seeing those pretty little yappers eyeing me when I hang my head out of the window, cooling it in the breeze. But this doggy hotel...I stayed too long when Grand Master left us to go where humans go when they are good. What's a dog to do? Humans will be humans!

FAMILY REUNION

One of the foundations of Henry's family was family reunions. The Stuart family reunion wasn't just a reunion for members of the Stuart family; it was a reunion of connected families who lived in a little town in rural Alabama called Claremont. The story passed down through the years was this: One Thanksgiving Day, during a gathering around the dining room table, Henry's grandfather, other family members, and friends began a conversation about family reunions. From that discussion, the idea of a Claremont Family Reunion was given birth. Interested families set out to organize the first Claremont Family Reunion during the second weekend in July. The children and children's children of those families have been gathering ever since. The reunion rotated its location based on where the host family was residing at the time. Such locations have included Detroit, Pittsburgh, Atlanta, Los Angeles, and more.

I was very impressed with the commitment to gathering espoused by the various families. One of the reunion's key events was the awarding of scholarships to high school seniors in the family community who were planning to attend college. This was a great way to promote the value of a good education and keep young people in the family engaged and poised to carry on the tradition of the family reunion for many years to come.

The next reunion was coming soon, and Henry and I were making plans to attend. The reunion was being hosted in Claremont, Alabama, the birthplace of many family members, which captured the attention of many, both in and out of state. Going back home was historic. I was excited about going, but I dreaded the thought of having to board Coco. The guilt that I harbored was sometimes overwhelming. This was one of those times.

He had not been himself over the last few weeks, as if he sensed we were getting ready to leave him again. My heart ached at the thought. Not only was he not as active, but his appetite was waning even more. (Whenever Coco didn't show up for a cookie, it was time to worry.) And I was worried. What if he got sick while we were away? What if the boarders didn't notice he was ailing? My mind raced with the possibilities and the what-ifs. I knew it was important to Henry that we go together, since this would be our first attendance as a married couple. But I was conflicted. I agonized about it for days. His vet tried to reassure me that he would be very attentive to Coco's condition, but I was still uneasy.

I hear Big Fellow and Lee talking about seeing family in a place called Alabama. Doggy hotel...here I come. I want Lee to be happy and go places, but I want her to be with me. Why can't I go too? I'm a good boy! What's a dog to do?

I know Lee is worried about me because she keeps checking on me whenever I slip away to take a little snooze. I'm snoozing a lot. But I'm tired a lot. Some days my get-up-and-go can't be found. I wonder if Lee knows I don't eat much. A little taste is enough. I'll get back to my old self...just need to catch up on a little sleep. Getting old is not for wimps!

I'm sure I can handle one more trip to the doggy hotel. Lee said after they leave me this time, they won't leave me again for a long time. She said we'll all go on a special trip when they get back. Music to my ears! I want us to travel like a family. We never went on a trip as a family when Grand Master was here. He was always too tired. I could tell when he didn't feel like playing with me. He would pull me close to where he was sitting and let me rest my head on his leg until both of us fell asleep. I miss Grand Master. Maybe going to the doggy hotel wouldn't be so bad. I'll think about all the fun I'll have when we go away together...Lee, Big Fellow, and Coco!

It was all set. Henry and I would attend the family gathering *after* the Claremont Family Reunion, but not the reunion itself. This would allow for less time away from Coco. He was still somewhat sluggish, and I didn't want to take any chances. Arrangements had been made to board him with his vet instead of the doggy hotel. I was relieved to know that his vet would be nearby if Coco needed medical attention.

The last few days were normal. Coco was more playful and would at least eat most of his cookie. I knew he always sulked a bit whenever I traveled, so I finally had to put my uneasiness aside. Coco's vet assured me again that he would take good care of him and call me if necessary.

Henry and I made plans to drop Coco off early that morning to get to Claremont before it was too late. It was about a ten-hour drive. I was glad to hear that we would gain an hour once we crossed the Alabama state line. Time was on our side.

I finally allowed myself to get excited about the trip. I looked forward to seeing all of Henry's family…and the food! There was always so much food whenever the Stuart clan gathered, so I could only imagine what the reunion would bring to the table.

A family fish fry was the most anticipated event. The fish fry was held after all the reunion events ended—the after-party, so to speak. One of Henry's aunts owned a house in Claremont. She stayed there whenever she traveled back home to Claremont from her residence in California. Other relatives lived there and took care of it while she was away. The home had a large backyard. Whenever the family reunion was held in Claremont, members of the extended Stuart family would leave the Claremont Family Reunion's closing event, which was generally over before noon, and spend the rest of the day at the Stuart family's fish fry. There were mounds of food: catfish, ribs, potato salad, corn, baked beans, collard greens, cabbage, macaroni and cheese—you name it. *Eatin'* was good at the Stuart family's famous fish fry! The backyard would be filled with laughter and people talking noise (as Henry would say), telling stories about their childhood experiences and catching up on each other's present lives. I was sure this year's event would be no different.

Henry and I checked into our hotel room first. We had reserved a room at a hotel not far from Henry's aunt's house in Claremont, along with other members of the family traveling down for the event. After getting refreshed, we headed out. Driving a short distance, we arrived a little earlier than planned, hoping to help set up tables and chairs outside as well as display the food. As other family members arrived, the rooms in the house quickly overflowed with the noise of laughter and greetings of hugs, kisses, and backslapping. Since the house was not particularly large, it was easy to meet and greet. It was a brutally hot day, which is not unusual for Alabama in mid-July—the peak of summer. So whenever possible, a lot of family members, myself included, huddled into a corner of the house rather than fight the intense heat outside.

Henry quickly introduced me to the family members I hadn't met as we mingled through the crowd. I was truly out of my comfort zone, but I worked hard to look at ease and enjoy the moment. Though I loved being around people I was familiar with, meeting strangers was always a challenge. For one thing, I was terrible at remembering names, especially during introductions at such a fast pace. Furthermore, what do you say to people you meet for the first time? "How are you?" It seemed so trite. But I managed to get through it all without tripping over someone's feet or falling on my face.

As we all made our way through the house, we headed toward the back entrance to the backyard. The food was already nicely laid out for everyone to help themselves. And boy, oh boy, did we help ourselves. Plates were piled high! Some family members swerved to keep from bumping into someone's plate. That would be a disaster! There was something there for everyone, except if you were concerned about your weight. But, by the size of those plates, no one at the Stuart family fish fry seemed

concerned about their weight! And if they were, the spread of
sweets, as we say in the South, would have knocked that idea out
of the park. Cakes. Pies. Cookies. Ice cream. I, for one, was in
dessert heaven.

BEGINNING OF THE END

After the feast, we all made our way to some comfortable spot in the house or outside to relax and revel in the joy of the food we had eaten. I hardly heard my cell phone as I chatted with members of Henry's family. Walking through the front room and out onto the porch to answer it, I noticed the number instantly: the vet's office. My heart pounded. It was Coco. I thought the worst.

"Mrs. Stuart, this is Dr. Barnwell's office. Coco is not doing well. We are very concerned. You may want to come home," the vet assistant explained before I could catch my breath.

"We'll be right there," I blurted out. Be right there? What was I thinking? We were hours away! Tears rolled down my cheeks. By this time, I had walked toward the end of the driveway to avoid being seen by anyone before calming down. Deep in my own thoughts, I did not notice Henry's brother Jerry standing behind me.

"I don't know what's going on, sis, but I know you need a hug." I let him give me a hug as we walked back toward the house. Jerry and I had hit it off the first time we'd met. We had grown close over the years. Henry and I often stayed with him and his family when we visited Detroit.

"I'll get Henry," Jerry said, walking ahead of me. By that time, Henry had missed me and was walking out the front door toward us.

"What's wrong?" he asked while putting his arms around me.

"It's Coco. He's not doing well. The vet is concerned."

"Okay, let's get ready to go."

"Are you sure? I can go alone. I can get a flight. You stay here with your family."

"No, we're leaving. We can head out early tomorrow morning."

"Okay. I'm so sorry to interrupt your family time."

"We were able to see the family, and now it's time to check on Coco."

Henry was as concerned about Coco as I was. For the first time, I became aware of how much he cared about my little Cocomo. It touched my heart.

We got on the road early the next morning as planned. It was a somber drive home. Neither one of us felt much like conversation. We listened to a lot of music and stopped only a few times to stretch and grab a bite to eat. It was about four in the afternoon when we reached the highway that would take us home. However, we detoured and headed to the vet's office. There was no time to stop.

I recall struggling to pull myself together before the vet brought Coco in for Henry and me to see him. I wanted to scream. My stomach felt sick, and I wanted to throw up. Henry kept his eyes on me. He sensed I was on the verge of falling apart.

After a short while, the vet's assistant came in with Coco sprawled across her shoulder. The vet had already given him a sedative to calm him. He was so weak and looked so scared. My heart sank when I saw him. His eyes carefully and slowly followed every move I made as I struggled to remove my jacket. Walking toward him, I gently maneuvered him into my arms and sat in a chair nearby. I held him close, saying nothing.

I can hear Lee's heart...wonder if she can hear mine.

The tears flowed freely, and we were all silent for a long while. The time I had dreaded the most had come. Even though this was not my first experience with putting a dog down, it was, by far, my worst. Coco was not just any dog— he was *my baby*.

Finally, the vet came in to see if we had questions before he administered Coco's lethal injections. I slowly slid Coco into the vet's arms and covered my face with my hands. I could not bear to watch him leave the room with my precious Coco. I felt so helpless, so confused. Was I doing the right thing? Coco's liver was failing him, but what if there was another treatment to try? Should I get a second opinion? These thoughts swirled around in my head like a whirlwind. I felt lightheaded and dizzy. I knew Coco was too sick, but not that sick. It seemed so sudden. He had given me fifteen years of unconditional love, and I didn't want him to spend his last days suffering. I took a deep breath and thanked God for Coco's life.

It was hard to believe that I had faced the same dilemma with Cliff. I remembered it vividly: Cliff had been rushed to the hospital three weeks beforehand, following our trip to Texas. He had reached the final stage of his battle with cancer and had been given literally hours to live. I was surrounded by his doctors, who were suggesting we administer morphine to make Cliff's transition more comfortable. I was in a state of distress and possibly denial, but I knew once morphine was administered, my husband's life would slowly end. *Dear God,* I prayed. *Is this the right thing to do? Please give me peace of mind about this.* What if we were interfering with the natural process of death? Were we playing God? So many questions boggled my mind. I knew Cliff was near death's door, but I wanted him to slip away into God's arms on his own...in God's timing. After talking with my pastor, who had called to check on me, and praying for guidance, it became clear to me that nothing could happen outside of God's timing, no matter the decision. I gave my consent for the doctors to proceed with the medication to ease Cliff's pain and make him comfortable as we waited for God to receive him home. Strangely enough, once that decision was made, a sense of calmness swept through my body as I settled in for a long night.

Again, I was praying for strength and peace as I waited for the vet to give Coco the initial dose of medicine. When the first injection was given, the vet's assistant brought Coco back in and gently placed his limp body across my lap. I had never felt such deep sorrow in my life. The hurt was unbearable. I raised Coco carefully into my arms to hug him close, and I began to wail. It came out of nowhere. *Dear God,* I prayed silently. *Help me.* This time, there was no tranquility. I could not stop the tears even if I'd wanted to.

As I sobbed uncontrollably, the vet's assistant stayed close, waiting for an appropriate moment to ease Coco away from my arms. When I finally handed him over to her, she carried Coco to another room, hoping to relieve my pain. It only intensified. Salty tears gushed down my cheek like a waterfall. I now wanted them to stop; they would not. I felt weak—trembling as if I were about to fall. Henry grabbed me and held me up, cradling me in his arms to comfort me and keep me from falling. I buried my face in his chest and sobbed even more.

It seemed like hours had passed when Henry slowly removed his arms, which were wrapped around my limp body, and walked me to the nearest chair. Looking up at him, I could see his eyes were wet. He loved Coco too. He steadied me into the chair. Henry had never seen me fall apart like that. I couldn't help wondering what he must have thought of my lack of control. But I was in too much pain to care.

"How do you want to proceed with the body?" the assistant asked.

"What are my options?" I could not believe I had to make that decision so soon.

"Some people choose to cremate. Others bury."

I was hesitant at first to cremate Coco because I couldn't think of any place special enough to release his ashes. I also wasn't sure if I could handle the reminder of his death by keeping his remains. It was all too soon, too totally unexpected. I couldn't believe my Coco was gone—July 23, 2013. I'll never forget the day.

The assistant must have understood my struggle. She left the room quietly and returned along with the vet. The vet explained that if I did not want to take Coco's remains home with me, he would be cremated and disposed of along with the other dogs. It all sounded so cold, so heartless. All things considered, I decided to take Coco home with me.

GRIEF REVISITED

I sat motionless, clinging to the tiny, chestnut-brown box that held Coco's ashes. Henry drove without saying a word, eyeing me occasionally to see if I was okay. It was surreal. I kept thinking how sad it was that I didn't have a special place to scatter Coco's remains. We had moved around too many times to nurture a favorite spot for him to rest in peace. One regret among many was not taking Coco to the beach. He would have loved it! It would have been a great place to memorialize him. But I never took the time. Maybe I was too concerned about those tiny grains of sand getting entangled in his wet hair. Coco hated it when I tried combing his hair, so I kept it cut short. Regardless, it was too late.

My beloved Coco had been reduced to a very small box of... dust. I couldn't get that thought out of my head. This was my first experience with the cremation of someone close to me. It was somewhat unnerving, since I generally had ambivalent views about cremation. I grappled with it spiritually. No matter what, my baby boy was gone. My grief was heavy.

"He was a dog—a pet," I kept telling myself. "How could this hurt so much?" Now I understood how Cliff felt about losing his dog and companion, Princess. The emotional pain was almost unbearable. I thanked God for not letting us loose Coco while Cliff was alive. It would have been too much.

I had many losses in my life, but none pierced my soul like losing Coco. I was utterly devastated! I began to think maybe my relationship with Coco had been unhealthy. I depended on him when I was alone and needed companionship. I talked out my problems with him. He was my confidante. I hoped he knew how much I loved him.

Perhaps I need to talk to my counselor, I thought. It had to be unnatural for anyone to feel this way about the loss of a pet. (I suspected I was not just grieving the loss of Coco.) I felt sick. But Coco was not just a pet; he was my family, my lifeline. His unconditional love kept me afloat, helped me survive many struggles. Sometimes during personal trials, I wanted to pull the covers over my head and sleep my troubles away, but Coco reminded me of my responsibilities. No matter how much I wanted to drown in my own sorrow, Coco wasn't having it. If nudging didn't get me out of bed, his nonstop barking would. I smiled every time I thought about it: Coco would cock his little head over his shoulder, as only he could, and bark like a maniac. I was forced to get out of bed and take him out to potty. And now Coco was gone. How would I survive without him? The smile didn't last.

The days passed. Henry tried to comfort me as best he could. I loved him for trying, but I was inconsolable. The worst part of all was not being able to share my sorrow with others. With Coco, I could talk through my tears all day and night. He was always there to comfort me. Now that he was gone, no one really wanted to hear about how much I missed him or how it felt not having him around. To them, he was just another dog. They only wanted to know when I would get another dog to ease my pain. Perhaps only a pet lover could truly understand my loss. I called it my invisible grief. I dared not express it publicly, for fear my friends would think I had lost my mind. Yet it never left my side. So I suffered in silence, longing for the day I could see another dog playing with his owner without feeling so sad.

Several months had passed, but my heart still sank every time I saw a doggy in a car with his nose pointing toward the sky, reaching for air from a partially opened window. I'd been afraid to fully open the window; Coco probably would have tried to jump to freedom, especially if a cute little terrier caught his eye.

Coco's death inevitably brought back memories of past losses, especially the death of my mother. My mind focused on the first time I'd seen her laid out in her coffin. My siblings and I had arrived at the family hour dreading the experience of seeing her lying there. Joyce and I—mostly Joyce—had made the funeral arrangements as best we could, given the weight of our sorrow. We'd wanted our mother's funeral to be a celebration of her life with a focus on the positives, and we knew we had to set the tone.

Everyone was still in shock, given the circumstances surrounding her death. Losing someone you love, especially from an assault, can trigger a complexity of emotions; anger—even rage—can take control of your thoughts and actions. Though I believed my mom's ex-boyfriend never intended to cause her death, his intention to cause her harm was undeniable. The pressure of that anger rested on our shoulders as we attempted to say goodbye. We were consumed with grief but determined to do what was expected of us.

The funeral director graciously escorted us from the family car to the front of the chapel and assisted us in lining up before entering the room where my mother's body lay. Just as we were about to cross the threshold of the door to proceed into the chapel, I saw this view of my mom in her coffin located at the top of the center aisle. Suddenly my body grew limp, and the world around me transformed into a soft, white light. All I could see was the stream of blinding light that extended from the door where I stood and my mom's coffin. I heard myself scream and felt myself falling over. Someone caught me and held me up. I remember slumping over in the back seat of the family's funeral car and wailing until I was able to slowly groan my way to silence. When I was able to walk again, a funeral attendant escorted me back into the chapel to say my last goodbyes to my mom. This time, I walked slowly toward the coffin, being held up by angels, closed my eyes, and kissed Ma on her cheek. Opening my eyes, I saw a smile looking up at me. Mom was finally at peace, and so was I—for that moment.

I didn't have Coco by my side at the time. I was sure he would have helped me get through my suffering. When Cliff died, Coco had a way of distracting me whenever I was feeling sorry for myself. I could count on him to bark his way to a potty break. Sometimes it took him so long to find his spot, I wondered if he really needed to go or if he just needed some attention. Nonetheless, I was eager to oblige. Besides, I didn't want him to stain my carpet again.

Speaking of taking too long to go, sometimes Coco circled a spot twenty times or more before getting in his "potty pose."

One day, I actually counted. It was the funniest thing! I must admit that it was tough on the days when I was pressed for time, and I was not amused. I needed him to get the job done so we could move on! Coco rarely accommodated. He could be stubborn at times—a real alpha male.

So many days, I found myself swallowed up with guilt. Why had I gone to the reunion? I should have stayed with Coco. I knew he wasn't himself. But it all happened so suddenly. I wished I hadn't left him alone so much or trotted him off for boarding when I traveled. Maybe I should have found a dog sitter. But I also wanted Coco to be around other dogs. He needed to play and run and chase other dogs. I always said he thought he was human. Maybe he needed a playmate. I hope he knew that I loved him and tried to take good care of him. The thoughts were terrorizing. They even invaded my dreams, disrupting my sleep.

As the days and weeks lingered, talking with my counselor helped me get back to some sense of normalcy. My heart still ached, but I was eventually able to find some comfort in seeing Coco's small box of ashes on the mantle of the fireplace—like he was still with me. In no time, I had created a memorial space, surrounding Coco's urn with pictures and toys and other mementos. It would take some time to heal, a lesson I had learned so well over the years. Yet I had not expected that having his remains close by would be comforting.

REVELATIONS

Months later, while watching television one night, I saw this commercial with a mother holding her child in her arms. Sitting at her feet was this beautiful dog that reminded me of Coco. I don't remember what I was watching or even the subject of the commercial. What I do remember is that it touched my heart in a profound way. Suddenly I started bawling. The tears were like a watershed. I couldn't believe it! "What is wrong with me?" I asked, looking up at the heavens as if expecting an answer from God.

I cried for a long while. Thankfully, Henry wasn't at home to witness another episode of me weeping. He had already experienced one too many. I tried to calm myself as I turned the channel to avoid seeing the commercial again. Shaking my head in disbelief of what had just happened, I had an astonishing revelation. Yes, I was crying for the loss of Coco, but I was also shedding tears for *the baby I had lost*. That thought came out of nowhere. I guess seeing a mother holding her baby, with her dog nearby, triggered something deep inside. A range of emotions flooded my heart. I became light headed. Burying my head in the pillow next to me, I cried until the tears stopped flowing. I did not want to go back. I had it all figured out in my head, and I didn't want to unravel the neat little package that I had wrapped so tightly more than twenty-five years ago. A wave of fear rushed through me. I was not ready to deal with this. "Oh my God!" I cried. "Is this your will for me right now?"

It was a cold day in January. I was at home recuperating. I remember the day well because it was the same day the space shuttle *Challenger* exploded in the sky seconds after takeoff. The television was on, but I was busy preparing lunch. I heard a noise and glanced over at the television screen, only to witness one of the most horrific tragedies in our lifetime. The television screen turned into a huge cloud of smoke penetrated by bright orange flurries of light. The onlookers were stunned. Television reporters were seen scrambling. I was frozen in place for a while. *Is this really happening?* I remembered thinking. It was all so shocking—so unbelievable. We later learned that all the people on board the *Challenger* had been killed instantly, including Christa McAuliffe, the first teacher astronaut to make the mission.

I'd had an abortion a few days before that awful day. No one knew of my loss, except Cliff, of course. I'll never forget the day I found out I was pregnant. I had scheduled an appointment to see my doctor for a routine visit. Diagnosed with fibroid tumors right out of college, I needed to be checked regularly to monitor their growth. One of my girlfriends was free to drive me, so I insisted Cliff not take time off from work to accompany me. I had not seen my friend in a long time, and we welcomed the opportunity for some girl talk.

The doctor's words exploded in my ears like a firecracker: "You're pregnant." I was shocked! I had no symptoms of a pregnancy. Cliff and I had been very careful since my pause in taking birth control pills. Having made the decision to take birth control pills early in our marriage, I had to take a break from the pills when the pain from the fibroids in my uterus returned. The pills were not helping my condition. So I was advised to discontinue them or take a pause for at least six months or longer. Realizing my confusion, the doctor explained that it wasn't unusual for women to become more fertile immediately after quitting the pill. This was apparently what happened in my case. So many thoughts swirled through my head, making me light-headed. *God, where are you?* I cried silently. I stood still for a long while, waiting for an answer. It never came.

After asking the doctor a few questions, I composed myself and headed out the door. I didn't want my girlfriend, who was patiently waiting for me, to know how distraught I was. I never told her I was pregnant. I wanted Cliff to be the first to know.

Cliff and I had planned it all out. We did not want a child until we were financially able to care for him or her. We knew what it was like to grow up in poverty. We vowed not to let that happen to our child. We were not ready, financially or emotionally, to care for another human being, especially emotionally. We were struggling to take care of ourselves at the time. Having a child seemed selfish and irresponsible. So we had agreed that we needed to wait. Besides, I didn't want to end up like my mom, having babies that I could not take care of. I did not want to be responsible for neglecting a child in the same way. I wanted my child's life to be different.

Nevertheless, I was crushed to hear Cliff say he was not ready. Neither was I, but I wanted to hear him say, "Let's keep the baby." Instead he said, "I'm not ready." I remember feeling a strong sense of abandonment. But I also knew that I wasn't equipped to be a good mother either. My inner child was still suffering from a lack of security and confidence. I needed to hear from God; again, I heard nothing but silence.

I got pregnant at the worst time in our marriage. Cliff was working part time whenever he could in addition to maintaining his full-time teaching job. At one point, Cliff's school district had been on strike, and the loss of anticipated wages derailed our budget. We were trying to catch up and maintain simultaneously. I also worked during the summer months to make ends meet. We didn't have a lot of savings, and we were curtailing our vacations.

I allowed all of those struggles to influence my decision to end my pregnancy. I know now that deep in my heart, I wanted to keep my baby, but I couldn't admit it. I let my fears overwhelm me: What if the birth control pills had damaged my precious child? What if Cliff and I couldn't take care of our baby and were not good parents? What if I got sick from the pregnancy and couldn't work—how would we manage? On and on and on. My mind soon became mush. I had convinced myself I had no choice. I began to feel numb. Cliff was not encouraging me one way or the other, which made everything worse. I felt all alone.

Although I was only a couple of weeks pregnant, my doctor suggested I make a decision as soon as possible to allow for the best possible outcome from a health standpoint. Days later, I made an appointment for the procedure. I felt empty and lifeless. I felt that way for a long time. No tears, no grief, no regrets.

After a few days of rest, I quickly got back to my normal routine of keeping busy. Cliff and I never spoke of the abortion. He was afraid of upsetting me, and I knew I would go crazy if I allowed myself to grieve. So we convinced ourselves that the best way to keep our sanity was to move on. We couldn't afford to wallow in self-pity. After all, we had responsibilities.

Things were never the same after that. Cliff and I acted as if nothing had happened. We threw ourselves into our work even more. We avoided any conversation that reminded us of what we had endured, and we never spoke of it with each other again. I closed the door of my mind on that chapter in my life and never looked back.

Three years later, I was told I needed a hysterectomy. My uterus had been invaded by fibroid tumors. It was too risky to remove them, and the pain was becoming unbearable. I felt as if my emotions, all the pain and the sense of loss, were sleepwalking. The realization that I would never be able to have another child was devastating. I handled the news the same way I dealt with the abortion: I buried my feelings so deep inside a little corner of my heart that they were unrecognizable—they did not exist—until I saw that commercial.

Here I was, more than twenty years later, swimming in my tears over a commercial. The irony was clear. I understood exactly what I had been praying to understand. Losing Coco had triggered an avalanche of suppressed emotions. His loss had catapulted me out of a state of denial, and I had landed in a sea of unresolved grief, an intermingling of grief for a dog I had subconsciously treated as my child. Losing Coco was like losing my child—a child I never knew—all over again. Except this time, I was lost in excruciating grief and sorrow.

This time, I didn't try to stop the tears. I wanted them to flow. I wanted to drown out those awful thoughts that had hardened my heart to the point of numbness. I wanted to flush out the fear, the coldness, and the shame that had kept me bound. I encouraged the tears by remembering those tender moments Coco and I had shared, as well as Cliff's cancer scare, Ma lying in her coffin, my beloved godmother's corpse being lowered into the ground, the unfamiliar face of my dying sister, my father's last breath. I wanted a waterfall. I wanted to be washed clean: *What can wash away my sin? Nothing but the blood of Jesus. What can make me whole again? Nothing but the blood of Jesus.*

It had become clear to me that I wouldn't be able to get past this pain and suffering without facing all the facts. It was time to dig deep. I didn't hesitate to seek professional help again. I sensed that my relationship with Coco was unique. It was not your usual pet-and-owner connection. I had allowed my subconscious grief and mourning for the baby I had aborted to be replaced by my love for Coco. I had transferred my feelings for my lost child to caring for Coco. Coco became the *baby* I never had. The feelings were real and raw. I embraced them with my eyes wide open. Losing Coco was a catalyst for a breakthrough— a breakthrough to the truth. A truth I had buried so deep in my subconscious. A truth I needed to face to be set free from shame, guilt, and suffering. Once again, even in death, Coco had rescued me.

TRANSFORMATIVE GRACE

More than a year had passed since Coco was called to doggy heaven. (Or as Coco would say, *the place dogs go if they have been good*.) I still had tearful moments, mostly when I walked through the pet aisle at the grocery store. For a while, I couldn't bring myself to push my grocery cart in that direction. If I had no choice, I would walk past the aisle with my head turned in the opposite direction or looking upward. I couldn't bear to see those doggy treats without thinking about Coco and how much he loved those cookies.

Whenever I yelled, "Cookie, Coco!" he was right there to retrieve his treat, standing on his hind legs and dancing around until the cookie was in reach. Grabbing it, he'd retreat to his favorite spot to savor its goodness. Coco loved human cookies most of all. Peanut butter was his favorite. Sometimes I would give in and give him a bite of my cookie by dropping a piece on the floor, as if by mistake. I couldn't let him think I was feeding him table food. He was always perched and ready for the kill, scurrying across the floor, grabbing the piece of cookie, and shooting out of the room before I could change my mind. I had memories…good memories that made me smile.

The leaves were starting to turn green, and flowers were bursting out of their seams. Spring was on its way. I recognized that I was on the road to recovery when my tears were transformed into joyful expressions of gratitude for what Coco and I had shared. I was beginning to feel like myself again, and I was so thankful for the memories I had of my life with Coco.

Henry and I had planned a busy summer, and there was much to do in preparation for our travels. I was looking forward to having fun again without feeling guilty. I sensed healing was imminent when I no longer felt like bursting into tears when asked, "Are you planning to get another dog?"

Maybe I *would* get another dog, but it was still too soon. Only I would know when I was ready. There was no rush.

I continued to thank God every day for gifting me Coco to help me in some of my darkest hours. I was grateful for the insights and the wisdom gained from caring for him. Someone once said, "Humans have the capacity to learn so much more from animals than animals can ever learn from humans." I don't remember where I heard it, but it rings so true in my case.

Coco was a wise and intelligent dog, as displayed in the ritual he performed whenever it was time to go outside for a walk or to potty. Strutting to the door, he'd always stop abruptly at the edge of the door, preventing me from opening it. Slowly, he'd lower his chest to the floor with his hind legs standing firmly in place, extend his front legs out as far as they would go, and hold what looked like a yoga pose for a few moments. Then, in one quick motion, he would leap up on all four legs. With his tail wagging like a windshield wiper in motion on a rainy day, Coco would look up at me, signaling he was now ready to go. I used to get so impatient with him until I understood that his repetitive behavior was important to his well-being. Coco knew in a doggy sort of way that stretching protected his joints, prolonged his endurance while walking, and gave him the energy needed to go the distance.

In time, I began to see the multitude of blessings God had poured into my life. I really didn't want to give Cliff a dog for his birthday because I wasn't sure he had the strength to take care of him. At that time, with all the responsibilities of Cliff's illness resting on my shoulders, the last thing I needed was doggy duty. Guess I was being a bit selfish about the matter. Fortunately, Cliff's brother (and the Holy Spirit) convinced me that getting a dog was not only the right thing to do, but it was a gift Cliff needed to provide some relief from his dreaded condition. Ironically, I needed Coco just as much or more than Cliff did. God had it all figured out. It was all in His plan for us—for me. Coco was not just *any* dog. He was our rescue dog, the dog we needed to see us through our season of pain and despair: lovable, funny, strong, loyal, patient, and courageous.

Life with Coco generated many teachable moments, like the power of forgiveness. No matter how many times I forgot to give him his medicine on time or was late getting home to take him to potty, Coco never held a grudge. In spite of my negligence, he always greeted me at the door as usual, wagging his bushy tail, letting me know he was happy to see me. Sometimes when it was difficult for me to forgive myself, Coco would curl up next to me and stare with those big, dark-brown eyes until I gently rubbed his head. When satisfied, he would flip over on his back so that I could rub his tummy. The look on his face was pure joy, reminding me that nothing was more important than love and forgiveness—giving it and receiving it.

Not just love, but unconditional love. Personal experiences and the observation of others have taught me that it is hard for us humans to sustain unconditional love, even when we want to. Insecurities soon weaken the fibers that weave it together. We falter. We forget. We need a show of love in return. Dogs are different.

Perhaps that's why Ma got pregnant without the means and support to take good care of us. Maybe she was looking for unconditional love, the love and attention she was so deprived of as a child. Ma loved us kids dearly, and we knew it. We felt it. But limited resources and her inability to find consistent work affected her ability to be an effective parent. She showered us with her love and attention when we were with her, and she left a legacy of love that has penetrated our lives in an extraordinary way. Even though we (my siblings and I) didn't grow up in the same household throughout our childhood, we love each other as deeply as we loved her.

One cold day in December before moving to the Carolinas, I was sitting on the floor in my bedroom facing the gas fireplace that had been recently installed. I was cold and tired—too tired to get myself ready for bed. As my eyes danced with the movement of the flames flickering around the synthetic logs, I did not notice Coco coming into the room. He snuggled close to me and rested his head on my leg with his eyes focused upward. Looking into his eyes, I saw nothing but love. I rubbed his favorite spot behind his ears to express my gratitude.

Coco could sense when I needed a hug without me asking for one. Not only did he know I needed a hug, but I didn't have to bargain with him in return for it. His love was pure and simple, the closest thing to unconditional love that I had experienced. I was thankful. Regrettably, we humans are not conditioned to give such a priceless gift to others so freely. Coco helped me see that it is truly worthwhile to try.

Experiencing life with Coco has given me a newfound sense of responsibility and appreciation for the animals in this world. They are God's creation and need to be treated as such. I have a greater respect for their environment and a lack of tolerance for acts of abuse that threaten their existence. Kudos to the many organizations devoted to their care.

At the heart of the matter, I owe Coco a debt of gratitude for saving my soul, even in his dying. Facing the grief and sorrow locked away in my heart from the loss of my unborn child was triggered by the emptiness and brokenheartedness I felt when Coco died. The grief was enormous. Subconsciously, I was mourning the loss of two, not one.

It's amazing that it took me so long to accept my abortion as a loss. I was in denial. I thought that if I didn't think or talk about it, it would go away. Intellectually, I knew from my counseling background that problems don't go away on their own. They stand back until the injured is ready to tackle them, but not without a price. Denial camouflages every situation, problem, and relationship that occurs thereafter to an unrecognizable state. It keeps us on defense when what we really need is the simple truth.

The truth is, I was ashamed about what I had done. I thought that since I had not shed a tear or felt remorseful, I had done the right thing. Otherwise, I wouldn't have been so calm about it. And if I had *not* made the right decision, I knew deep down that

God would forgive me. Only He knew my heart and my help-lessness. So I *kept it moving.*

Many people looked up to me and counted on me to make the right choices in life. I felt the pressure. I was held in high esteem by many of my friends, family, and coworkers. But I felt like I had deceived them, like I was not the person they thought I was. My inner child convinced me that I was not as honorable as people perceived me to be. For so long, I struggled with how to be more authentic, more genuine (even though I thought I was), so that others could see the real me. If I were to be judged, I wanted to be judged on the facts, experiences that have shaped who I am today—not on impressions.

Squarely confronting my guilt and shame has allowed me to accept my imperfections and my flaws. Most importantly, I am grateful for God's forgiveness. Even though I had not mourned my unborn child, I seldom prayed without asking God to forgive me for my sins, known and unknown, and renew a right spirit within me. I believed to my core that if I asked for forgiveness in the name of Jesus, I was forgiven.

The trials of life have taught me to believe in the promises of God. I am holding on to his promises of forgiveness for dear life. As God has forgiven me, I have been able to forgive myself and have reconciled myself to my powerlessness—knowing that in my weakness, God gives me power. Consequently, my faith in Jesus Christ has grown tremendously, and my relationship with God is so much more fulfilling.

So what do we do after God forgives us? I was enough of a biblical scholar to know that God expects us to gain wisdom from our mistakes and wrongdoings. There are consequences to face, lessons to learn. "Maybe that is why I suffered so many deaths," I reflected out loud. "Maybe He needed to teach me in His own way the power of grieving and how to mourn." God wanted me to learn about grace and mercy.

Struggling to comprehend, I was well aware that even in my wrongdoings, God saw fit to bless me. From start to finish, God had a plan. I believe Coco coming into my life and loving me unconditionally was part of that plan. Grieving his loss helped me find the courage to give myself permission to mourn my un-born child. My deep and extended sorrow was a manifestation of grief not grieved, a grief that had been buried so deep it was almost unrecoverable.

So where do I go from here? Though this question has not been answered to my complete satisfaction, there is one thing I am sure of: God wants me to help someone else who might be struggling with death and grief, someone who might be suffering an overwhelming loss, a loss denied…an invisible loss. Someone needs to know: being at peace about your past can promote free-dom in your future.

To be clear, the reflection of my experiences is not a judg-ment or commentary on abortion. I wholeheartedly believe that this decision rests with a woman, her God, and her doctor. Essentially, only Jesus is judge and jury of our actions. And as scripture teaches us, *we all fall short of the glory of God.* When considering the noise that pollutes the air today, abortion has become a hot topic. Ultimately, I believe that women must not be silenced to shame in regard to how the law of the land applies to and affects our health and well-being.

The revelations that have come forth from my experiences with death, dying, grief, and denial are complicated but simple:

I cannot fully live unless I can find peace with dying.

I cannot find peace with dying unless I allow myself to heal.

I cannot heal unless I give myself permission to grieve.

I cannot give myself permission to grieve unless I am willing to name that grief.

As I strive for ways to restore my soul and renew my spirit, I find peace in knowing God is in control of my life. He has guided me through many days of darkness, always leading me toward the light—His light. His light has taught me that suffering is temporary but necessary to help us appreciate the goodness of life. If we let it, suffering will deepen our faith and strengthen our resolve to mourn our losses. God Almighty might not move the mountain, but He promises to hold our hands as we climb—reaching for the top. Knowing this, we can rejoice and have faith that on the other side of pain and sorrow are eternal joy and peace.

I will continue to honor and cherish the memories of those I have lost and continue to lose. And with God's grace, I will continue to mourn the loss of my beloved Coco...until complete healing comes.

EPILOGUE

Few people journey through life without experiencing grief and suffering. People I admire the most are those who have endured extraordinary suffering resulting from circumstances beyond their control: a young child in an abusive home; someone dealing with a debilitating disability or terminal illness; a husband or wife mourning the loss of a spouse. Some might remember the epic scene in the movie about the life of Tina Turner when Tina gains the courage to fight back and walk away from her abusive marriage. She had an epiphany moment: she was ready to take back her life against all odds. Think of Dr. Martin Luther King Jr., who suffered police brutality, verbal abuse, defamation of his character, and ultimately, the loss of his life. And no one can forget the grief and courage on full display as Jackie Kennedy held the head of her fatally wounded husband, President John F. Kennedy, in her lap after his assassination. Moments like these have been most inspirational and have compelled me to persist when life events became unbearable, even suffocating.

Most of all, imprinted on my heart is the suffering of Our Lord and Savior Jesus Christ, who died a sacrificial death for our sins. The pain and suffering He endured on the cross are incomprehensible. Jesus Christ *defined* suffering. Accepting suffering and the grief, shame, guilt, and pain often associated with it is a critical response to trauma in our lives if we want hope. Not accepting it can lead us to despair and destruction. In many ways, this story is my testimony to the promises of God when we put our faith in Jesus.

I hope the episodes of my life as they unfold in this book will inspire someone to confront the losses in their life with courage and boldness and embrace the love that God so freely gives to walk in His Spirit. As followers of Christ, we must own and share our stories to help bring light to others, particularly others who don't know Him.

Acknowledging and accepting grief that can accompany an abortion is often troublesome because of the guilt and shame it fosters. Either we don't recognize the grief, or we don't want to admit that it exists. Further, the spotlight that shines on women who have abortions today makes it even more burdensome for us to own our past and confront our fears. The power of the belief and influence of others can overwhelm us to the point of desperation and denial. Nonetheless, owning a loss forces us to face our convictions and honor our truth—to be set free.

I hope my story will inspire someone who is suffering from shame or guilt to remember the power of God's forgiveness and His redeeming love. If nothing else, I hope that it will remind someone who is struggling with whatever loss—a job, a marriage, a death, an abortion, a friendship, a child given up for adoption, a family connection, a church home—that we belong to the family of God. He will, after you have suffered, transform you and give you peace. Wherever you have fallen short in over-coming your grief, shame, guilt, pain, or suffering, you can be strengthened by grace that only Christ can give. It is yours for the asking.

But he said to me,
"My grace is sufficient for you,
for my power is made perfect in weakness."
Therefore I will boast all the more gladly
about my weaknesses, so that
Christ's power may rest on me.
2 Cor 12:9 (NIV)

ABOUT THE AUTHOR

Dr. Wilson is a retired secondary school counselor who dedicated much of her life mentoring and encouraging young people. She's one of the founding board members of a foundation which awards annual scholarships to eligible high school seniors attending college or a vocational school and has published *A Walk on the Beach: A Sacred Space*. Dr. Wilson attributes her success in life to her faith, supportive family members and friends, and the many divine interventions that paved her way.

Dr. Wilson resides in Indian Land, South Carolina with her husband. In addition to writing, she enjoys listening to music, attending concerts and theatrical performances, and traveling.